1986

Fires of Love
Waters of Peace

Fires of Love
Waters of Peace

PASSION AND RENUNCIATION
IN INDIAN CULTURE

LEE SIEGEL

UNIVERSITY OF HAWAII PRESS • *Honolulu*

Library of Congress Cataloging in Publication Data

Siegel, Lee, 1945–
  Fires of love—waters of peace.

  Includes bibliographical references.
  1. Sanskrit poetry—History and criticism. 2. Erotic
poetry, Sanskrit—History and criticism. 3. Religious
poetry, Sanskrit—History and criticism. 4. Amaru—
Criticism and interpretation. 5. Śaṅkarācārya—Criticism and interpretation. I. Title.
PK2916.S47 1983   891'.21   82–21767
ISBN 0–8248–0828–2

For Patricia

aho tvaddhṛdisthitenāgninā dīptiḥ
aho tvatsambhāṣasalilena mārdavaṃ

Contents

Dreaming before fire, dreaming before water, one
knows a kind of stable reverie. Fire and water have
a power of oneiric integration. . . . In following
them we adhere to the world; we take root in the
world.

GASTON BACHELARD

Preface

THIS IS A REVERIE before fire and water, an attempt to follow fire
and water as symbols of antipodal experiences: love and peace,
passion and renunciation. I have written here about Amaru, a
Sanskrit court poet, and Śaṅkara, a saintly Indian philosopher,
as exemplars of antithetical ideals, spokesmen for divergent and
yet intertwined traditions: an aristocratic, literary tradition in
which the erotic sentiment was extolled and in which the world
of the senses was affirmed; and a philosophical, religious tradition in which the goal was liberation from the world through a
denial of the senses and a suppression of desire. My concern has
not been with Amaru and Śaṅkara as actual figures who lived in
the seventh or eighth century, but with them as types, as they
have been understood and formed in the Indian imagination.
They are personas in a history of Indian reveries.

A significant portion of this book deals with Sanskrit erotic
poetry as it is typified by the Amaru collection. Because the Sanskrit poet wrote not so much to express his personal feelings as to
perpetuate and celebrate the sensibilities of his cultural heri-
tage, I have felt free to consider these poems as scenes from a
collective dream. The poems tell of the beginnings of love and
of its fading, of the joys of union and the sorrows of separation,
of hope and disenchantment. The poet depicts innocent girls
and passionate ladies, devoted husbands and faithless rogues. In
some of the poems love is a sophisticated game of both skill and

chance; in others love is a genuine reaching out for human warmth and intimacy.

By examining the poetry in the light of the consecrated philosophy expounded by Śaṅkara, the major proponent of the Advaita Vedānta system, I have juxtaposed the attitudes reflected in the poems with religious values. As with the poems of Amaru, the teachings of Śaṅkara express not so much his individual ideas as they do a tradition, an ancient and persistent school of philosophical speculation. While there have been many such schools in India's intellectual history, Advaita Vedānta (with its assertion that there is but one sacred reality, an absolute which is nondual) is a powerful current in the mainstream of Indian thinking. I have not attempted to analyze the philosophy; rather I have used it to give an impression of the force and flow of the larger river. In so doing I discuss certain works attributed to Śaṅkara not because he actually wrote them (in many cases he did not) but because they have been traditionally ascribed to him and can, therefore, reveal something of the Indian conception of the wisdom of a holy teacher. The Śaṅkara and the Amaru of this book are composites formed of many Śaṅkaras and many Amarus. Respectively they embody religious and secular ideals. The ideals eclipse the actualities, endure, and acquire a truth of their own. Historical data could be misleading. This is a reverie on reveries.

The two prototypical figures, the renunciate and the lover, as well as the ideals they represent, come together in a traditional legend in which the spirit of Śaṅkara is said to have entered the body of Amaru in order to experience sexual love while remaining chaste. The revealing legend is a focus of this book. Amaru and Śaṅkara seem to illuminate one another, even to need one another. Passion and renunciation generate each other. The diastolic flexings of the heart, expansions of feeling and expressions of desire, seem to demand systolic responses of equal force and measure, contractions of feeling and retractions of desire. The reconciliation is not in the moment but in the rhythm: the continuous and regular pulse of the human heart.

The harmonization of contrary impulses is the concern of this book both as a recurrent theme in Indian culture and as an issue which is at once intimately personal and mysteriously universal. This study, then, is not meant for the specialist, the Indologist as such, but for the reader interested in discovering how universals can manifest in one cultural context. India is a metaphor.

In translating Amaru's Sanskrit poems into English I have tried to convey, through a variety of rhetorical strategies, something of what I believe to be the mood or tone of each poem. All translation is interpretation; when my interpretations or strategies have moved me away from the content of the original, I have included a literal rendering in the notes.

I am deeply indebted to Kenneth Langer, as well as to Rama Nath Sharma, for many erudite comments upon my translations, and I am very grateful to various people—particularly Richard Gombrich, Wendy O'Flaherty, and C. Milhaud—who extended interesting and helpful comments along the way. The cover photograph was kindly provided by Prithwish Neogy. Research Fellowships from the American Institute of Indian Studies and from the Center for Asian and Pacific Studies (University of Hawaii) gave me the opportunity to write this book. From the beginning Patricia Crosby has offered sensitive perceptions and intelligent reactions; she should know that she has my loving gratitude.

are one and the same. This reality, inner and outer, hidden and ever present, awaits the revelation which comes when one finishes with existence and longs for the waters of peace. It is for that anxious heart that Śaṅkara speaks:

> The words of Śaṅkara, bestowing liberation,
>   will prevail!—
> To those who wander in the course of life,
>   lost in the wilderness, thirsting for water,
> Tormented by the incandescent anguish,
>   the sun's flaming rays,
> His words reveal the joy inspiring oneness
>   of *brahman,*
> A nectarous ocean, so very near.[1]

Amaru sings for those who delight in the flames—lovers who have discovered a mirage so vivid that they do not care about its insubstantiality. Enamoured phantoms drink nectar from each other's lips and seek a different oneness. The poet, in his own way, is as venerable as the philosopher. The Sanskrit poet was called *kavi*—originally a "seer," a priestly one. Gifted with insight and the holy voice of praise, he could invoke and confront sacred powers within and without and hear mysterious rhythms and reveal magnificent patterns. There were Indian aestheticians who equated pure experience of poetic sentiment with the experience of the oneness of *brahman*. The aesthetic moment was understood as a sacred moment, an eternal instant typified by a joy of insight into that which is.

Love, the sentiment and the god, is the power invoked in the poems attributed to Amaru. The poems are conventionalized erotic pictures of the enchantments of the world and the subtleties of human feeling. Moments from all the phases of loving and courtship are crystallized and savored. These poems, collected together as the *Amaruśataka,* form a portrait album of lovers, a portfolio of intricate miniatures executed with detachment and with wit.

> Fire and water are enemies and yet
> moist heat is the source of everything—
> concordant discord is suited to creation.
>
> OVID

CHAPTER ONE

Invocations

AMARU AND ŚAŃKARA embody antithetical ideals—the man of the world and the man beyond the world, the sensual aristocrat and the saintly ascetic. The former, utterly fascinated by the splendid multiplicity of things, celebrates the delicate illusions of life; the latter, burdened by the intractable tedium of things, penetrates appearances and shatters the gross delusions of life. The holy man dreams of awakening; the lover dreams of dreaming. The philosopher is a *voyant;* the poet is a *voyeur:* both *see.* Indian culture absorbs both visions, both revelations—the world of experience is at once esteemed and deprecated, adored and feared. Engagement in the world, in all of Amaru's lovely pleasures, is an ideal and yet the idealization is cautious, for enjoyment is ultimately justifiable in Indian traditions only as a preliminary to renunciation. Finally the goal, in this life or one to come, must be the conquest of desire, a triumph over flesh, an extinction of the fire.

Śaṅkara is venerated in India as a religious reformer, a spiritual master, a teacher of a primary truth: beneath phenomena, behind this inconstant world of the senses, there is an unchanging reality, an absolute peace, a pure joy, sacredness itself, the very godliness of the gods, *brahman.* It alone is real. And beneath the empirical self, behind the name and form, the persona, there is an unchanging, absolute, sacred identity, *ātman.* *Brahman* and *ātman,* the universal and the personal absolutes,

The words of Śaṅkara would be recited or read and then pondered by teachers and students, mendicants and philosophers, in forest retreats or caves, in monasteries and temples. The poems of Amaru would prevail in courts or bowers, on picnics or at trysts. They would be sung or read and then discussed by charmed connoisseurs, ladies and gentlemen, at parties with laughter and wine. The experiences of love, refined by sophisticated courtly lovers, further refined by the poet, were distilled to produce a verbal intoxicant, deliciously sweet, to be relished by people of taste.

The Sanskrit word for poetry, *kāvya,* is a qualitative rather than a formal term describing any work of prose or verse which is infused with a particular and conventionally delineated *rasa,* an aesthetic mood, flavor, or sentiment. *Rasa* can be fully savored only by people who, through many births and diligent study, have been trained to take a transcendental pleasure in the universality of the sentiment. They are *rasikas,* literary gourmets, who relish the good taste of poetry—the flavor produced through a harmonious blending of lovely images, melodious words, and sublime ideas. Poetry aspires to displays of beauty and intelligence while philosophy aspires to truth and wisdom. The philosopher discriminates between the real and the unreal, between what is *brahman* and what is not. The *rasika* discriminates between the poetic and unpoetic, between what has *rasa* and what does not.

Amaru's poems are informed with the erotic *rasa,* the mood or sentiment of love. They reflect not so much a personal erotic experience as a cultural appreciation of the erotic essence, an aesthetic experience of a universal. The universal and the individual converge in the Indian perspective. The poet expressed collective emotions, institutionalized ideals, feelings which the aestheticians and rhetoricians had established as tasteful and true. Similarly Śaṅkara's philosophy is not so much his philosophy as it is a reiteration of ancient precepts. The philosopher is original only in the sense that he aspires to return to sacred Vedic origins. The teachings reflect the attitudes esteemed by a priestly group; the poetry reflects the attitudes of an aristocratic group. The poet as a learned celebrant of sexual love was at once a teacher and an entertainer with an important position in the life of the court. He validated the impulses and indulgences of a class of people who were dedicated to the delights of the sensual world in the face of a religious system which asserted that one must seek liberation from the world. The poet performs; the philosopher reforms.

It is not possible to know who Amaru was, when or where he lived, whether he composed or collected the *Amaruśataka*. He may have lived in the sixth, seventh, or eighth century. Perhaps he was a professional scholar in the service of a king or perhaps he was himself a king.

Śaṅkara may well have been a contemporary of Amaru. The numerous legends about him form a detailed hagiography. He is thought to have been born in Kerala, a member of the priestly Nambūdiri caste. Having mastered all the sacred scriptures with ease at an early age, he renounced the world, became a sannyasi, an "abstainer" or "renouncer," and while still a child began his travels throughout India. During this random pilgrimage he expounded upon scripture, debated other teachers, preached, performed miracles, converted the wayward, and founded spiritual centers.

In one of these legends Amaru and Śaṅkara converge. Śaṅkara, the ascetic of absolute chastity, was engaged in a philosophical debate with the Vedic ritualist and householder Maṇḍana Miśra, whose wife challenged Śaṅkara with questions about the erotic arts and sciences. Admitting that true wisdom must include an understanding of all aspects of life, the pious celibate asked to be excused from the debate for a month in order to master the theory and practice of love. Granted leave, Śaṅkara flew over the earth by means of magical powers accrued through yoga. Meanwhile Amaru, identified in the legend as a king of Kashmir, died on a hunting expedition in the forest. Finding the body of this king, who possessed a hundred beautiful wives, Śaṅkara prepared to leave his own body and enter the form of Amaru so that he could study at first hand the manifestations and dynamics of sexual love. The philosopher assured his uneasy disciples that he would be able to indulge in erotic activity without taint because he who is without desire for pleasure cannot be burned by the fires of lust. "How can he who realizes that the world is mere appearance," Śaṅkara asks, "be affected by anything?" And so King Amaru of Kashmir appeared to come back to life, appeared to return to his palace, and appeared to indulge in love games and erotic experiments with his lovely wives and mistresses. He played dice with them setting sexual favors as the stakes, drank wine with them, kissed and caressed them with what appeared to be exuberance. Śaṅkara, who was, we are told, "eternally immersed in the joy of the absolute," appeared to experience the transient joys of carnal love. And, according to the legend, in the name of Amaru he wrote a poetic work displaying his mastery of the sexual sentiments and erotic arts—the *Amaruśataka*. The holy man then abandoned the body of the king and returned to win his debate with Maṇḍana Miśra.[2]

The legend stamps the collection with an invisible imprimatur. The poems become innocent by association, acceptable to the chaste as dispassionate memos on theoretical erotics. The poems are, of course, in no way ascetic; yet they might be, in some sense, religious. While it was the goal of sannyasis, inspired by the teachings of saints like Śaṅkara, to experience the sacred through asceticism, it was the goal of *rasikas,* inspired by the words of poets like Amaru, to experience the sacred through aestheticism.

Both Śaṅkara and Amaru were worshipers of Śiva, and in the vast mythology of that god—Śiva is the erotic ascetic, fire and water—there is implicit fusion of the passionate and renunciatory impulses. At once ferocious and gentle, Destroyer and Creator, slayer of demons and lover of the goddess, Śiva is an exemplar of power: sexual power, martial power, and religious power, the power of yoga. Amaru invokes the power in a benedictory poem describing Śiva's assault on Tripura, where

three demon brothers who attained dominion over the universe
through their ascetic practices ruled the heavens from a city of
gold, the sky from a city of silver, and the earth from a city of
iron. The gods implore Śiva to attack the three cities, to destroy
the universe that it might be recreated. With an arrow of fire,
the angry flame of his sexual energy stored and augmented
through the austerities of yoga, Śiva destroys the three citadels
merged as Tripura. The demons and their women perish in the
conflagration:

> Like offended mistresses crying
>   out against eager advances,
> Like piqued ladies trying
>   to resist seductive glances,
> The lovely weeping women
>   of Tripura tremble with despair;
> Like a fervent, unquenched lover
>   tugging robes, pulling hair,
> Like an ardent lover clinging,
>   impassioned, burning to the soul,
> The lustrous fire, a lustful lover,
>   consumes the women whole:
> May the lustral fire,
>   the flame of Śiva's dart,
> Burn away your sins forever
>   to purify your heart![3]

The beginning of the poem is a conventional description of
court ladies offended by a roguish lover's inconstancy, a typically
playful and innocent erotic scene. The lover falls at his beloved's
feet, pulls at the edge of her garment, tries to embrace her while
she seems intent on repulsing him with tears of pique in her
eyes, an attitude designed to enhance her allure. Then a mythic
reality asserts itself. It is not a lover seducing a woman, it is fire
burning flesh. The figurative flames of passion suddenly become the literal flames of destruction. As the image comes into

focus, what was erotic becomes grotesque. Behind love's pleasures, then, there is something dreadful and cruel. For Śaṅkara
there can be no embrace, no lover's touch, no moment of passion that does not rage with this destructive fire. Desire is the
"enemy of the world"—every desire is an "unquenchable fire."[4]
The world of the senses is a forest in flames.

Fire, the energy which expresses itself sexually in love, heroi-
cally in battle, religiously in sacrifice, coalesces creation (pro-
generation and digestion) and destruction (conflagration and
cremation). In the Vedic rite fire carries all sacred offerings to the
gods and digests it for them. Fire is the medium through which
the divine and the human make contact. The fire is started by
friction—symbolically the phallus churns in the vulva faster and
faster until there is a spark and the sacrificial, sexual, fire sacred-
ly burns. Maṇḍana Miśra wields fire: the erotic fire as householder, the sacrificial fire as ritualist. Śaṅkara's antipathy to
Maṇḍana Miśra is antipathy to fire.

Śaṅkara invokes not the fiery Śiva, the qualified deity, the
god who rules over the illusion, but Śiva as *brahman,* the
unqualified reality, neither ferocious nor gentle, neither erotic
nor ascetic, neither lover nor warrior. The philosopher, whose
name is an epithet of the god, expresses his identity with the
god as the absolute principle within and without:

OM
i am not
mind, soul, ego, memory
not
ear, tongue, nose, eye
sky, earth, wind, fire
I AM ŚIVA I AM ŚIVA
AWARENESS AND JOY[5]

Behind the unreal multiformity of the universe there is neither movement nor desire, neither gender nor love, neither
birth nor death, neither god nor goddess. And yet as the unreal

arises out of the real, the relative arises out of the absolute. *Brahman* and *māyā*, the illusion which is this world, become the metaphysical equivalents of the god and his *śakti*—Śiva's power which separates from him to manifest divinely as the goddess, cosmically as nature, humanly as woman. She is beautiful and terrible, a source of sustenance and deprivation, of tender love and painful death. The energy is sweetly erotic and darkly destructive. Amaru prays for her protection:

> her eye
> reflections of the light
> shimmering fingernails
> stretching the bowstring
> her eye
> a black bee restless
> thirsting for the flower
> ornamenting her ear
> her eye
> may it watch over you![6]

The arrow of the goddess slew the virile buffalo-headed demon who oppressed the universe with power attained through austerities. The goddess manifested as a celestial nymph to lure him, seduce him, weaken him, and prepare him for the kill. The ambivalence of the goddess, of nature, of woman, pervades the imagery of the invocatory poem. The seductive glance, conventionally compared to an arrow of love, is counterpoised with a literal arrow of death. The poet uses a word for "bee" which also means "lover." The demon is enticed by the nymph as the bee is enticed by the flower ornament. The nails of the goddess can be sharp weapons of torture in battle or splendid implements of pleasure in embraces. Dark and light, soft and sharp, movement and stillness, submission and aggression, all are tightly juxtaposed. The convergence of opposites strains, is tense, and holds for only a moment against the pull of the bowstring. When the goddess lets go, releases the arrow, the image falls apart, the demon dies: poetry into silence, life into death.

Amaru's benedictory poems, linking the erotic aspects of the god and goddess with their heroic aspects, their sexual power with their power to protect, provide a justification and sanctification of the erotic mode of life. Sexuality is godly activity, sacred energy. But sexuality is dangerous, too, for erotic joy has a dark bond with something mysterious, terrible, and deadly. The erotic life is fraught with peril, then, for desire binds one to the aching round of rebirth and redeath from which, in the Indian context, one must inevitably seek release. While the poems in Amaru's collection celebrate the joys and wonders of love in all its phases, beneath the delight one senses a touch, however slight and hidden, of fear and profound sadness. Behind the jubilant songs of Amaru one can almost hear the faint austere whispers of Śaṅkara. And while the teachings of Śaṅkara profess detachment and transcendence, there are traces of an ecstasy that can only come from some species of desire. Gods are worshiped in the monasteries which Śaṅkara is said to have established, and the teacher came to be credited with the composition of numerous devotional hymns to the god and goddess in a variety of forms. This seeming contradiction of Śaṅkara's doctrine is justified with explanations that through devotion to personal manifestations of the sacred one may gain access to the impersonal *brahman*. The relative leads to the absolute. Śaṅkara expresses his detached attachment to a deity who is immanently transcendent, a very real illusion:

Hymn to Śiva
Essence of the Veda

I love the killer of Love, the one, great god—
Lord of tethered beasts, destroyer of evil, almighty,
Clad in an elephant skin, supreme,
The river Ganges flowing within his topknot, the ascetic's
braids of matted hair.

I praise the mighty lord, the god with five faces,
    eternal joy,
The great lord, god of gods, demon killer,
Supreme lord of the universe, whose body is ornamented
    with ashes. . . .

I take refuge in him, paramount, pure, beyond duality,
Unborn, eternal, cause of causes,
Auspicious Śiva, alone, light of lights, beyond darkness,
Realization of *brahman.* . . .

The world comes from you, god, cosmos, killer of Love,
And in you the world abides, compassionate lord of all,
And in you destruction comes,
And in your phallic nature, Hara, you are lord of the world
    —manifested in everything, the quick and the dead.[7]

Śiva as *brahman* is no-thing; Śiva as he begins to manifest is
every-thing. *Brahman* is neither male nor female; but the primary manifestation of *brahman* as the qualified Śiva is both
male and female, the primal androgyne who divides into Śiva
and Śivā, god and goddess. The god is dependent on the goddess, the *śakti* or "power" by which he creates, preserves, and
destroys the universe. And she is as paradoxical as the god, at
once a young bride and mother, at once woman and the very
ground and essence of being:

> Bride of Śiva!
> You are mind, space, wind and the fire
>   which has wind as its charioteer;
> You are cosmic waters and earth;
> You transform yourself into all things
>   and when you do, nothing is beyond;
> You are, by your nature,
>   Awareness and Joy![8]

Devotion suggests separation, distinction between subject
and object, but Śaṅkara admits no separation or distinction—
the words with which he expresses his adoration come from her:
"My paean is but a rite of salutation made to the ocean with its
own waters. . . ."9 Worshiper and worshiped merge like water
and water, waters taken from the sea to be offered back to the
sea in gratitude. Devotion is but a means whereby the subject is
drawn closer and closer to the realization of its identity with the
object. For Śaṅkara separation is the fundamental illusion. The
sannyasi is he who, feeling the pain of separation, seeks the
blissful reality of union. The lover is no different. Amaru seems
to parody Śaṅkara's philosophy and mock hymns to the goddess
attributed to the saint. The lover, separated from his beloved
with no care about *brahman* or anything other than his beloved,
comes to the same understanding as the holy man:

> She, she, she, she is right here,
> She, she, she, she is right there;
> She is far and yet near,
> She is everything and everywhere:
>> Am I Amaru, the suffering lover,
>> Or Śaṅkara working undercover?10

As the legend suggests, Amaru and Śaṅkara, antithetical
types, ultimately converge. Śaṅkara's sober rhetorical question—
-"How can he who realizes that the world is mere appearance be
affected by anything?"—arises out of a disenchantment with the
sensual world and yet it permits thorough enjoyment of it.
Before enlivening Amaru's body Śaṅkara explained to his fol-
lowers that "for him who is firmly established in the supreme
teaching of Vedānta the commandments and prohibitions of the
śāstras have no application."11 There is little difference between
priestly renunciation and aristocratic indulgence. Both are amor-
al. Using a word which can mean either "pearl" or "liberated
one," the poet is able to reconcile erotic delight with asceticism,
to justify sexuality with wordplay:

> Those pearl necklaces are playing
> On the breasts of loving girls;
> Since "pearls of wisdom" is a saying,
> It must be wise to act like pearls.[12]

The poet wrote for a social group devoted to finding pleasure in the world through love, courtship, and all sensual delights. They were able to do so in a cultural milieu in which the ultimate goal as formulated by the priestly caste, was liberation from the world through overcoming desire, attachment, love. The revelation that ultimately all is illusory, that in the end nothing matters, inspired and gave license both to rigorous asceticism and to wholehearted passion. The waters of equanimity and the fires of exuberance come from the same source. The very gods that teach and exemplify modes of liberation give themselves up to extravagant lust—Brahmā commits incest with his daughter, Viṣṇu makes love to sixteen thousand women, Śiva violates the wives of the Pine Forest Sages. Religious renunciation and erotic annunciation converge.

Amaru and Śaṅkara are further reconciled in the hagiography with the explanation that not only was Amaru really Śaṅkara in a guise to learn of love but also Śaṅkara was really Śiva in a guise to teach men the path to liberation. And Śiva, in turn, is only really *brahman* in a guise to be known and worshiped. The world is a complex interplay of illusions, guise upon guise upon guise, trickling waters and flickering flames.

The sannyasi strips away the facades, discards the ornaments, to find behind the masks a nameless, formless, silent reality. The poet delights in the masks. With all the fervor of the ascetic in his quest for the real and the joyous, the lover searches for the unreal and the sorrowful. Love needs to be unreal in order to be real. It needs to sadden in order to bring joy. The world and the heart that feels the world's power are paradoxical. Illusion is the only truth in a world or heart that is ever changeful. Things come and go with the moment and the eon. And the fleeting world of love is, at best, like rain:

> First monsoon rains enrapture,
> Rains dripping through the roofs
> Of hovels tattered by slashing,
> Swirling, windy torrents; within
> Women, busy at their chores,
> Are cooled, their breasts are wet.
> Raindrops glisten on white flower petals
> And faintly mark the sand. . . .[13]

The waters dry out, the fires die down. Lover and ascetic, poet and philosopher, courtier and holy man, pass by and the sands are faintly marked.

Now therefore, while the youthful hue
Sits on thy skin like morning glow
And while thy willing Soul transpires
At every pore with instant Fires,
Now let us sport while we may.

What should we do but sing his praise
That led us through the watery maze
Unto an isle so long unknown
And yet far kinder than our own.
                                    ANDREW MARVELL

CHAPTER TWO

Beginnings

SANSKRIT POETRY achieves its effects through the dynamics of
suggestion and resonance. A small scene suggests a vast drama,
an incident resounds with a fuller story. All the actions and feelings of lovers from the first moments of longing through all
aspects of separation to final union are classified and explained
in the canons of poetics and erotics. A particular moment in the
process of love suggests the whole; the instant insinuates a continuum. In four lines, following a strictly defined metrical pattern, the poet condenses a phase of erotic experience into a
highly contracted poetic image. The *rasika,* knowing the conceits, conventions, and categories, reexpands the image and
extends it beyond its specific references. The poetic process, this
compression and amplification, occurs between the poet and the
rasika. They are interdependent. The poem is understood, the
resonance is heard, according to the theoreticians, when the
rasika is as sensitive, learned, and inspired as the poet.

Just as the sannyasi values certain deities as epiphanous forms
of *brahman,* the *rasika* values depictions of erotic particulars as

manifestations of a universal *rasa,* the aesthetic essence of love. Love has its epiphany in nameless, conventional lovers. They are never unique and their love story is always the same. It begins with a longing which leads to union which, in turn, leads to a separation. Then there is a new longing and an inevitable reunion. The lovers participate in the established pattern; they manifest the universal rhythm.

Passion in its inception is kindled, the poets and aestheticians say, through clandestine glances, fired like arrows into the heart. Anxious, hopeful, and burning "at every pore with instant fires," a young girl, the possession of her father, longs to be possessed by a lover and to feel herself changed into a woman. The pain of transformation is cherished as sweet misery. The first sexual union is ritual initiation into the mysteries of love. The pubescent stirrings are selfish, but the poet is charmed by the selfishness of young lovers on the brink of discovering their ardor. A young girl, freshly infatuated, is embarrassed because her friends have betrayed her feelings to the man she loves. She cries out in fear that love ripens only in secrecy:

> No longer can I trust my dear friends;
> No more can I even glance at the one I love—
> I'm ashamed—he knows what fills my mind;
> How adept people are at deciphering love's gestures,
> How quick they are to laugh, to joke, to tease.
>> Where can I turn? Where is there refuge?
>> Mother! The fire of love dies within me.[1]

If the loving girl does not find union with her lover, if the fires of love die in her heart, she will perish with them. The treatises on erotics and poetics describe the phases of passionate longing. Weeping and sighing, anxiety and depression, are symptomatic stages in the fatal disease, love:

She weeps
Amidst her loved ones;
Her parents fear for her,
Her friends feel the misery.
The melancholy spreads about her—
The sorrows of separation are shared.
She is weary now of sighing, of breathing.
But rest easy. Soon, so soon, she'll taste the joy
Of death.[2]

The poet seems to parody the ascetic who is able to overcome sorrow and attain emancipation. This "joy of death" is the supreme beatitude, the final extinction, achieved through renunciation. The young girl, Amaru promises, can enjoy the goal of Śaṅkara through passion and attachment. Passion attains what dispassion strives for.

The final stage of love, death, is never depicted in erotic poetry. The deep sorrow of love is easily remedied with kisses. The sadness of first love, the pain of hungering for union, is as transient as the joy of union. The poetry of Amaru, like the philosophy of Śaṅkara, is infused with a sense of the ephemerality of feeling.

Strict conventions, repetition of conceits, ornate figures of speech, and erudite allusions often create a distance. The poems do not generally inspire empathy—it is the poet's skill rather than the lover's feeling that is, very often, on display. The poem is as illusory as the world. Unreal lovers move through it. Illusions, as Śaṅkara insists, become delusions when they are taken as realities. But illusions, Amaru implies, taken for what they are, can be as enchanting as the wives of the poet-king whom Śaṅkara seemed to embrace.

The traditional ideal for the young male of high caste was to become a *brahmacārin*, a student of the Veda making strict vows of chastity to protect him from delusions and provide him with defenses against the onslaught of sexuality. He was removed from the world of women and placed in the home of an intellectual and moral preceptor, a guru, under whose supervision he would study the sacred texts. According to the hagiography Śaṅkara was initiated into this period of studentship at the age of five, shortly after the death of his father. By the time he was eight years old he had mastered all Vedic knowledge. The scriptures, according to the author of the legend, "when interpreted by Śaṅkara, revealed a new significance, just as a beautiful girl shines with added luster when united with a worthy husband."[3]

In adolescence the girl is prepared for domesticity, for the husband who will give her luster; she is ultimately fulfilled through sexuality. The boy is prepared for an ultimate renunciation of sexuality, for a time when, after living the life of a householder, he will find his ultimate fulfillment wandering, nameless, homeless, and utterly detached and dispassionate. Chastity is the ideal for both boy and girl, but the girl's chastity is an ornament enhancing her sexual appeal whereas the boy's chastity is an armament against that appeal.

Śaṅkara epitomizes the spirit of the *brahmacārin*—the emphasis is always on the perfection of continence and the refinement of learning. Continence is considered an aspect of wisdom. According to the hagiographer, Śiva, lord of the world, felt it necessary to incarnate on earth as Śaṅkara for the express purpose of "stamping out all traces of sexuality in himself."[4] Asceticism was so natural to Śaṅkara that when his mother was pregnant with him the line of hair on her stomach was said to look like the staff which sannyasis carry.[5]

While the boy was being trained in detachment, the girl was being trained in attachment. The traditional ideal for the young female was the artless girl, gentle, intelligent, and obedient. The poets and rhetoricians describe her as innocent and coy in both love and anger. The appeal of the girl is in the tension between her innocence and her passion, her hesitancy and her desire. Her glances awaken and reveal love. She is all eyes, dark eyes, pupils dilated with erotic anticipation:

your eyes
                languidly turned
love-wet
                suddenly closed
following him
                bashfully glancing
fixed on him
                pouring forth
heart-intentions
                the love . . .
tell me
                innocent girl
who is he
                the lucky man
you watch
                with your eyes?[6]

Young lovers, kept apart by parental propriety, are articulate
in the language of eyes. At once timid and bold, awkward
and agile, adolescent lovers hide their desires as they exchange
glances and winks in the presence of elders. Love in the presence
of elders, like *brahman* in the world, is simultaneously con-
cealed and revealed. Authority is the enemy of love and the
friend of renunciation. While the *brahmacārin* submits unques-
tioningly to his spiritual preceptor, for whom he begs alms and
from whom he takes his instruction in truth, the young girl is
ever defiant of the venerable elders who support her. Love is
always furtive and rebellious.

Swept away by rivers of love
    (swelling floods of their desire),
Torrents dammed by their elders
    (propriety all parents require),
Close they stand, anxious but still
    (hiding passions, restraining sighs),
Lovers drink nectars from the blossoms
    (the love that pours from lotus eyes).[7]

The poems, like the gestures of lovers, subtly suggest more than can be said in good taste. The poet, like the young girl, must convey passion without transgressing the bounds of what is proper. As social propriety, in the interest of order, creates the need for a lover's language, so aesthetic propriety, in the interest of order, creates the need for a poet's language, a discursive system of conceits and conventions, mannerisms and formalities. This language of suggestion is traditionally explained with the metaphor of a bell. The poet strikes the note and there is a resonance, a ringing persistence in which we feel the lingering power or charm of the note. The slight gesture, the fleeting moment, can contain vastly more than itself. The philosopher too endeavors to find the vastness of the moment. He too strains to describe the indescribable and to use words to transcend words so that the mind might find its way beyond the mind. Poet and philosopher, Amaru and Śaṅkara, respond to the world with language, a chaste and sacred language that can be used tenderly or aggressively. Sanskrit, the language of both writers, is traditionally esteemed as perfect and eternal. It is perfect when describing *brahman* and perfect when describing the bashful smile of a young girl. Language captures the world and transforms it. The Sanskrit language, the language of men, is both weapon and enticement, a defense against the world, which is female, or an access to it.

The male, human or divine, young or old, wise or foolish, is, in the Indian context, the perpetual victim of the female: nature, woman, the goddess. The poet unlike the holy man—Amaru unlike Śaṅkara—can delight in victimization, in the deadly wounds of love, in the splendid humiliation and suffering of passion. The poet legitimizes sensuality with language. Poetry makes love acceptable.

The sentiments of first love render the experienced man as vulnerable as the young girl. He recollects the beginning of desire. The spirit of love, before it became embodied, moved freely over the landscape of imagination. Retrospectively the pain of expectation seems more joyous and substantial than the joy of union. Sexual climax is anticlimactic. Poetic nostalgia is a thirst for a more delicious thirst, a sentimental memory of an innocence that longed to lose itself. For the poet, the mere thought of a young girl whom he has begun to love brings sacred exultation, the supreme bliss of extinction of which the philosophers speak. Through an ambiguous use of language Amaru equates the joy of love at first sight with Śaṅkara's religious beatitude:

> When loving glances first afflict the heart
>   and passions grow ardent,
> When there are plots, plans and messengers'
>   words are flowing—
> Then even to wander on the road
>   near her house brings
> Sacred exultation—and never mind
>   the joy of making love.[8]

Love weakens the male just as it gives the female strength. Love effeminizes. It turns things upside-down and inside-out:

> She's the one who's young, so why am I so shy?
> She's the one who's supposed to be afraid, not I!
> She's the one who bears the burden of her breast,
> So why am I the one who needs to take the rest?
> Her bottom is another burden she must bear,
> And yet I can hardly move from here to there!
> It's really quite amazing, the way that love assaults,
> Making *me* suffer *her* charms as if they were *my* faults![9]

Passion causes a reversal. The mature man is powerless; the young girl has mastery over him. Renunciation too instigates reversal. While a *brahmacārin* begging food for his guru, Śaṅkara came upon the home of a woman so poor she was able to give him only a single piece of fruit. Moved by the woman's generosity, Śaṅkara sang a hymn to Lakṣmī, goddess of prosperity, and at once solid gold pieces of fruit began to rain from the

heavens. The now prosperous woman bowed in gratitude to
Śaṅkara. The reversal is made—the supplicant becomes the do-
nor, the indigent becomes wealthy, the maternal figure receives
sustenance from the young boy. Both reversals transpose subject
and object and are prefatory to their identification. This identification is the aim of both asceticism and love.

Śaṅkara's prayer seduces the goddess. The celibate has a power over the female that the sensualist does not know. The ascetic
courts the goddess, the feminine aspect of the divine, to possess
her. But then she who has been seduced is ultimately abandoned. The devotional ascetic, the Śaṅkara to whom the hymns
are attributed, becomes the dispassionate ascetic, the Śaṅkara to
whom the philosophical tracts are attributed. Like a young girl
forsaken by her lover, the goddess is discarded by the philosopher. She is finally only an aspect of *māyā*, deceitful as any
female, to be abandoned for the sake of *brahman*, truth.

After Śaṅkara completed his studies and left the house of his
guru he maintained his vow of chastity and thereby remained
invulnerable to the feminine allure of the material world. As
love weakens the male and gives the female strength, the chastity of the male weakens the female and empowers the male,
enables him to keep the seminal energy within himself. Returning home, Śaṅkara found his mother too frail to make the long
walk to the river where she bathed. By singing another hymn to
the goddess, Śaṅkara was able to divert the course of the river so
that it flowed near his mother's house. The potency of praise,
the power of the ancient Vedic seers, can divert rivers or bring
showers of golden fruit.[10] Praise wins the favors of the goddess
just as flattery wins the favors of young girls.

There is a paean to the Ganges attributed to Śaṅkara in which
the Ganges is at once river and woman, heavenly and worldly,
chaste and erotic, mother and maiden, transcendent and immanent. The teacher exclaims that he who is enmeshed in the phenomenal world, the egoist or sensualist, need only sing the
hymn and his sorrows will fall away. He will be guided through
the "watery maze." The devotee is to redirect passion from

human manifestations of the female energy to the polymorph-
ous manifestation flowing through the three worlds from
beyond:

> Goddess, mistress of the gods, Lady Ganges!
> Savior of the three worlds, sparkling current,
> Stainless river meandering from Śiva's topknot. . . .
>
> Your waves are white as pearls, the moon and snow.
> Remove the burden of my sins—
> Transport me across the ocean of being with mercy.
>
> He who has tasted your pure waters,
> He indeed has attained the highest state.
> Yama, King of Death, cannot see the one
> Who is devoted to you, Mother Ganges. . . .
>
> My lady, take away this foolish bundle of mine:
> Passion, sorrow, grief and evil.
> Precious necklace of the earth, best of the three worlds—
> You are indeed my refuge in this world! . . .
>
> It would be better to be a turtle or a fish in your water,
> Or even a miserable lizard on your banks,
> Or even a wretched dog-catcher near to you,
> Than to belong to a king's family living far away. . . .
>
> There will always be joyous liberation for those
> Who have devotion for the Ganges in their hearts.
> This hymn to the Ganges contains the essence of
>   existence. . . .
> It was composed by Śankara, the servant of Śankara. . . .
> May the sensualist, his mind fixed on her, recite it![11]

In her manifestation as the cleansing river connecting heaven,
sky, and earth, the female energy is benign. This image of her as
a link between the three worlds gives mythological expression to
the ontological connection between the real and the unreal, the

transcendent and the immanent. The renunciate swims against the current; he conquers the river. The lover flows with the current; he surrenders to the girl.

As Śaṅkara used language descriptive of a woman to depict the Ganges, Amaru uses language descriptive of the Ganges to depict a woman. And as the encomium is recited to win heavenly rewards and joys, the flattery is recited to win amatory rewards: the favors of the young girl. The lover goes to his lady as a pilgrim goes to the Ganges:

> —the slender girl: the autumnal Ganges—
> her cheeks, the banks
> and her earrings like the poacher's traps;
> her brow, his bow;
> her eyes, two birds
> fluttering with love.[12]

Superimposed upon the image of the young girl, her ears adorned and her glance cast at her lover, is the image of the Ganges in autumn, the time of year when wagtail birds are said to mate in rivers. Through the superimposition death and sexuality, the aggressive impulse and the instinct to survive, are juxtaposed. A transparent huntsman, his traps set for the mating birds, is ready to fire arrows, weapons suggestive of the assault of the god of love. Lovers are as endangered as wagtail birds by their sexual desires. Lovers risk death because love, as Śaṅkara says, attaches us to this unreal world of death.

According to the Sanskrit aestheticians a metaphor or simile occurs when a poet, seeing two distinct images, superimposes one upon the other. Superimposition is fundamental to the poetic process which transforms nature into an aesthetic reality. The superimposition of the river onto the girl intensifies her presence and gives her a reality. Superimposition is an aspect of a poetic gnosis which gives rise to understanding, delight, and the experience of *rasa*. But the aesthetic ideal is the ascetic anathema. According to Śaṅkara superimposition is the source of ignorance and despair; imagination is the obstacle separating us from the one true reality: the experience of *brahman*. The poet and lover impose; the philosopher and renunciate expose. "Just as a rope is imagined to be a snake . . . so one's true nature is thought by fools to be the body. . . . Just as a person, out of confusion, perceives a snake, instead of the rope, so the fool sees the world without knowing reality. When the real nature of the rope is known, the appearance of the snake no longer abides. So when the substratum is known empirical existence becomes empty."[13] Śaṅkara's example is chosen carefully —seeing snakes we are afraid of harmless ropes; seeing ropes we are too confident amidst serpents. Śaṅkara advises: "Do away with superimposition!"[14] Neither the philosopher nor the poet, the ascetic nor the lover, accepts the phenomenal world. Śaṅkara describes the ontological reality underlying empirical reality; Amaru describes the aesthetic reality overlaying empirical reality. For both, reality as we ordinarily perceive it is unreal.

Superimposition changes not only the world, the object of perception, but also the perceiver, the subject of perception. The distinction between subject and object is, according to Śaṅkara, a symptom of ignorance. There is no self and no other; there is only the Self, the One. Our projections onto the world, our misperceptions of the world, result from the notion of an empirical self, a subjective individuality. And just as the subject forms objects, objects form the subject in a reciprocal delusion. We are transformed by the ways in which we transform the world; we are imagined in the ways in which we imagine the world. Amaru is sensitive to this process of mutual transmutation:

My friends, you must realize:
When my lover nears, I become all eyes;
I don't understand, my dears:
When my lover speaks, I become all ears.[15]

Transformations are caused by superimpositions which are in turn, according to Śaṅkara, caused by memory. Looking at a rope, the deluded man remembers attributes of a once-perceived snake, qualities which are projected onto the rope, causing fear in the man—a fear which then leads to further superimpositions, transformations, and fears. Various Sanskrit words for "memory" suggest and often mean "love"; the god of love, Kāma, is also named Remembrance. Love is both the cause and the effect of transfigurative superimposition. As the lover looks at his lady her thin waist evokes the memory of a Vedic altar which is narrow at the middle, and at once her breasts become ceremonial urns on that projected altar:

> Deer-eyes and well-formed thighs,
> The lady's body is a sacred altar,
> Slender at the waist; her breasts,
> Two golden fonts, overflowing with
> Holy waters for the consecration
> Of our Lord—the mind-born god
> Of love.[16]

The image of a religious devotee before an altar sprinkled with water in an initiatory ceremony is superimposed upon the image of a lover anointed with perspiration from his beloved's breasts. Superimposition, imagination, and memory can sacralize the erotic impulses and transubstantiate lovers in the realm of poetry. In the philosophical context, however, there is access to the sacred only in a direct and immediate perception of reality, one which annuls the world. Memory is transcended. The beloved is not, nor can she be, dear or sacred for her own sake, but only for the sake of the absolute reality invested with her form. She is dangerous because she inspires remembrance and love, projection and deception.

The beloved is *māyā*, a concealing appearance veiling *brahman*. When Śaṅkara insists that *brahman* alone is real, he means that "it" alone is unchanging, unqualified, eternal and infinite. *Māyā*, because "she" is changeful, personal, temporal

and finite, is unreal. *Māyā*, that which evolves the empirical
world and conceals or distorts reality, spreads deceit and ignorance. Śaṅkara delineates the dynamics of *māyā* with the example of a magician performing a trick. We are deceived both by
the power of the magician and by our own ignorance. As we witness the conjured illusion we are indeed "taken in"—we become
an extension of the illusion. We are part of the trick until we
understand how the magic works—knowledge is liberation. The
cosmogonic magic show may amuse the poet but it is a horror
show, full of deadly tricks, to the renunciate. "The man who
sees variety, who is deceived by *māyā*," Śaṅkara warns, "goes
from death to death."[17] *Māyā* is the death we mistake for life—
we are born only to begin dying, and when the process culmi-
nates in death we are born again only to begin dying once more.
Through the fiery course of redeath, we die our life, a living
death, until *māyā* is obliterated. The sannyasi breaks away from
māyā; he struggles to overcome her. "*Māyā* can be destroyed by
the realization of pure *brahman,* one without a second, just as
the mistaken notion of the snake is removed by discrimination
of the rope."[18]

Māyā is the ontological manifestation of the same force which
is humanly incarnated as woman. Every woman personifies the
beguiling unreality of worldly things. The young girl learns to
perform the tricks of love, to make the mannered moves in the
amatory game. The rules require her to be bashful and coy:

> The first love-trick:
>   he tugged her robe
> she bowed her face modestly
>   he reached for passion's embrace
> she pulled back gently
>   unable to speak
> she looked to her friends
>   their smiling faces—
> the new bride gasped,
>   so deeply shy.[19]

Shyness, real or feigned, is the standard opening move. It is an invitation to play the game. The man enters the game according to the script of erotic conventions. He seems audacious, sexually imperious, accomplished and artful. But the game has a paradoxical structure—offense is defense and defense is offense. She who seems blushful and bashful is very often, beneath the surface, desirous and wholly erotic. And he who seems self-assured and lusty is perhaps not always quite so. The woman is interiorized; her feelings and motives, like her genitals, are hidden. The man is exposed. The woman's seduction of the man is subterranean—it finds surface expression in a contradictory form, the man's seduction of the woman. The man is seduced into seducing. The dichotomy which permeates empirical reality, the dichotomy between what seems and is, is enacted by lovers in courtship. When the poet describes a young girl coerced to the bed for loveplay it is perhaps not that the woman needs to be lured but that the man needs to lure. His pleasure is as much in strategizing the conquest as it is in enjoying its spoils. And her joy is in surrender:

> Touching the drawstring, her beloved whispered,
> "You'd be lovely even without this bodice. . . ."
> Making excuses, friends departed, delighted
> With the gladness in the bride's eyes, the eyes
> Of the smiling girl on the edge of the bed.[20]

The girl's second move is to postpone lovemaking—to find an excuse, real or not, to delay union in order to make it all the more gratifying. A foreplay of gestures and signals, or pretenses and games, sustains the seduction. The woman bears the responsibility for the hesitancy which prolongs and heightens desire. Menstruation, normally repellent, becomes charming in that it postpones sexual union and therefore serves desire:

He begged a kiss,
winking, lip trembling:
she stood away, back
from the bed of love,
covering her face
with a fluttering shawl,
cheeks full of smiles,
earrings, clustered blossoms,
slowly shaking, shaking
her head ("no, no,")
it was in bloom—
the sanguinary flower.[21]

The young girl's modesty becomes an ornament adding to her loveliness. It enhances a beauty which is seen not so much in natural grace as in refined artfulness. The loving woman is intricately painted with cosmetics. Adornments are worn even during lovemaking. The beauty of girls, like the beauty of poetry or the world, is an external quality, a brilliant surface, a dazzling superimposition, the splendid beauty of *māyā* which is so dreadful to Śaṅkara. Beauty must be renounced for it is full of death. Śaṅkara explains that one must respond to lovely things as one naturally does to "crow shit."[22] Amaru, however, responds to the normally repugnant menstruation with the same delight that one naturally feels for a blossoming flower. Love invents the beauty of the world; renunciation points to its deceit. This theme, the notion of the hideousness of beauty, finds mythological expression in the recurrent motif of the demoness disguised as a lovely woman. The god or hero is he who can penetrate the feminine guise, the surface of nature, the world-illusion, *māyā*. The beautiful is dreadful because it leads to involvement in what is insubstantial.

When the goddess, Pārvatī, danced alluringly before Śiva to entice him out of his asceticism, the god was unmoved. But when she retired to the forest, replacing the sandal unguents on her body with ashes, and devoted herself to ascetic austerity, Śiva went to her with desire. Chastity is deeply seductive and full of power. *Brahmacārins* use it for power, for liberation; young girls use it for seduction, for love. The ideal girl maintains a delicate balance between artfulness and artlessness, impetuosity and hesitancy, bashfulness and daring. When she believes that her lover is asleep she takes the opportunity to do what her sense of modesty does not normally allow. His sleep permits her to be at once brazen (she passionately kisses him) and coy (she does so when no one is aware of it). But when she impulsively kisses her beloved she suddenly realizes that his sleep, like her modesty, is a guise:

> when she saw the room was empty
> She rose softly from the bed;
> long she watched her husband's face
> Not knowing his sleep was feigned;
> fearlessly she kissed him and at once
> His cheeks were bristling with delight—
> modestly she bowed her head and
> Her laughing lover kissed her.[23]

There is an interplay between the dreamed and the actual. All human action is a fleeting dream, a phantasmal appearance. Śaṅkara explained to his disciples, in the legendary biography, that he could experience sexual union in the body of Amaru without blemish for the same reason that there is no merit when one performs sacrifices or austerities in a dream.[24] Levels of illusion, dreams within dreams, appearances within appearances—all are interwoven in the fabric of *māyā*. Śaṅkara explains *māyā* in terms of dreams. A dream is an individual's *māyā*, a private experience illuminated by an inner light. Waking consciousness is the universal *māyā*, a collective experience illuminated by an outer light. Just as an individual has a personal experience in dark, dreamless sleep of an unqualified and impersonal essence, so there is a universal experience, unqualified and impersonal, illumination itself, the experience of *brahman* as *brahman*, beyond experience. Phenomenal experience is but a shared dream, a collective pretense. One pretense causes another which causes another. We wander in a maze of deceptions, a hall of mirrors, a chimerical labyrinth.

Love is the quintessential pretense, an elegant lie which can transform copulation into courtesy, biology into culture. Nothing is ever direct. A man, desiring to embrace a woman, pretends he must explain something to her in private; the woman, wanting to be embraced, pretends to believe. Her innocence is a pose. In order to boast of the embrace to a friend, she pretends to complain. And the poet pretends to be the girl as he speaks with her voice. He pretends to be describing an actuality:

> He invited me to a lonely spot—
> "I have to tell you something."
> Innocent-hearted and trusting,
> I sat close to him, attentive:
> He whispered in my ear,
> He smelled my mouth,
> He pulled my braid,
> He drank, dear friend,
> My lip's love-nectar![25]

In the refined and mannered game of love a young girl's candor is a maneuver, her artlessness an art. Without difficulty, hesitation, or sentimentality the young girl can fool her husband or lover, her family or friends. Parents see their shy daughter offer a pomegranate seed to the house parrot and an image of innocence is superimposed upon an opposite actuality—the girl is trying to choke the bird so that it cannot announce the sounds of her passionate lovemaking:

All night the parrot listened to the bride and groom;
In the morning he recited with the family in the room.
"Oooooh, ahhhhh, oooooh, ahhhhh," thus did the parrot
    speak
Until a ruby earring was placed before its beak.
"Polly wanna nice red seed?" so sweetly asked the wife;
The jewel made Polly quiet, for it ended Polly's life![26]

Pretending sweet indulgence the girl is able to subdue the parrot, a bird which in Indian mythology is the vehicle of Kāma, the god of love. Through her intractable cleverness and cunning charm, woman, the embodiment of *māyā*, attains mastery of love's domain. And she dominates her lover, enraptures and ensnares him, with her beauty. He is at once victim and devotee:

> these eyes—wide-shimmering
> those breasts—heavy-firm-raised
> her walk—burdened-langorous by
> her massive hips—my dearly-beloved:
> enchantress![27]

The young girl is an "enchantress" (*jīvita-hāriṇī*), a double-edged compound that might be understood both as a beloved woman, "gladdener of my life," and as a murderess, "taker of my life." She both enlivens the man and makes him go "from death to death." It is in this sense that she incarnates *māyā*, the universal sorceress. The poet and lover are willing to be spellbound and take the murder with the gladness. The philosopher and the renunciate must abandon her for the sake of peace.

Traditionally, after leading the life of a *brahmacārin* a boy would become a householder, renouncing his chastity in order to pursue material and sensual pleasures. For a poet this would mean graduating from the study of the Veda and beginning the study of poetry. According to some rhetoricians the study of poetry surpasses Vedic scholarship—while both lead to fulfillment of life's highest aims, the study of the Veda is dry and difficult whereas the study of poetry is pleasurable and relatively easy. Amaru and Śaṅkara simply make different choices.

Following the orthodox ideal a young man would continue his participation in society as a householder until late in life when he would be expected to withdraw once more from the world in order to enter a hermitage. And then, for the sake of liberation, there would be the final stage: the complete renunciation of the world, the life of the homeless sannyasi. Contrary to the ideal and against the expectations and hopes of his mother, Śaṅkara

wished to move directly from the first stage to the last, to give
up being a *brahmacārin* in order to be a sannyasi.

After returning home to his mother Śaṅkara grew restless,
according to the hagiographer, anxious for his mother's permission to become a mendicant. But she was determined to find a
wife for him. During this period Śaṅkara's reputation spread
and the hymns composed by the chaste young boy were soon
sung throughout the land. The king of Kerala invited the boy to
join his court as a poet and pandit under his lavish patronage.
Śaṅkara explained that he had no use for riches or the sensual
pleasures of the court, the milieu in which Amaru presumably
prospered. The child preached renunciation, and the king, recognizing the presence of the divinity within Śaṅkara, fell in
obeisance before him.²⁸

For Śaṅkara there is but one aim, liberation, and but one way
to live, as a sannyasi. Wealth and affection, power and ritual,
friends and lovers, family and community appeared to him as
but "drops of water on a lotus leaf"—transient and insubstantial, full of pain and misery:

> Who are you?
> Where are you from?
> To whom do you belong?
> Who is your beloved?
> Who is your son?
> This world, this life,
> Is all too mottled.
> Consider the truth—
> This is it, my brother:
>
> Don't be proud of
> Wealth, friends, youth—
> In a moment Time
> Destroys it all.
> Realizing that,
> Completely renounce illusion,

Set yourself upon
The path of *brahman*.

Abandoning love,
Anger, greed, delusion,
Realize "I am the Self."
Fools have no
Knowledge of the Self;
They are held in Hell
And tormented.

Dwelling at the foot of a tree,
The abode of a god,
Sleeping on the ground,
Clad in an antelope skin,
Renouncing delights and property,
Dispassionate,
Who would not be happy?

Control the breath;
Withdraw the senses;
Discriminate between
The changing and the changeless;
Be completely absorbed in prayer;
Be attentive, vastly attentive!

Life is as very fleeting
As water on a lotus leaf,
So very unsteady.
Learn it—the world
Is uniformly tormented
With disease and pride,
Struck with grief!

Devoted to lotuses, the guru's feet,
Be liberated immediately from the world.
By restraint of the mind and the senses
You shall witness God established in your heart.[29]

Will the change. O be inspired for the flame
in which a thing withdraws from you,
    a thing which glories with transformations. . . .

To the still earth say: I flow.
To the rushing water speak: I am.

RILKE

CHAPTER THREE

Journeys

SANSKRIT RHETORICAL TEXTS classify poetry which has the amorous flavor, which conveys the erotic sentiment, into depictions
of lovers' union and depictions of their separation. The separation of lovers is subclassified according to the cause of the es-
trangement: it can be voluntary, caused by the woman's feigned
or sincere jealousy or anger; or it can be involuntary—imposed
by family, as in the poems of first longing, or the result of an
important journey the man must take. The reason for the travel
is not given. Perhaps it is for business or battle, the result of fate
or an obligation or a curse.

These classifications of love and love poetry reflect a larger
Indian epistemological impulse. All aspects of life, erotic and
domestic, social and religious, all phases of experience, are cata-
loged and categorized, subcategorized and sub-subcategorized
compulsively and obsessively in the *śāstras*, the learned compen-
diums and treatises which have regulated all of Indian life. The
implicit assumption in this vast literature is that to name is to
know. To measure, designate, and set in order is furthermore to
create. The world is established not out of nothing, but through
dividing up what already exists and giving functions to the
parts.

The poetry does not attempt to reveal love through explorations of new emotional domains for the sake of fresh discoveries. Rather it proceeds by adhering to the established categories, following the detailed charts of the well-mapped terrain. The poems illustrate the classifications. They provide a taxonomy of love as a primal force that has been civilized, a chaos that has been ordered. The world of love is created through delineating the phases of emotional experience—the poetry reflects not so much the feelings of the poet as the structures with which the culture has created the world.

Sanskrit love poetry is never tragic—the categories do not permit it. The aestheticians decreed that the *rasa* would change from the erotic to the pathetic if one of the lovers were to die. A poem depicting death cannot be charming; and poetry, like love, is invented precisely to render charm to life that it may be endured in joy. And yet there is, in the poems which illustrate lovers separated through the man's journey, a genuine melancholy. Because the separation is only temporary certain poetic delight can be taken in their anxious parting and in the subsequent grieving for the distant beloved: ultimately the consummate sorrow serves to heighten the pleasure of reunion. Delight could not, however, be tastefully taken in the mourning of a widow: death is a pollution. And yet the poems about lovers' journeys borrow from the sadness of bereavement for the dead. One painfully longs for a "dear departed one" who has gone on a journey as if that journey was into death.

The departure of the man, leaving the woman at home and taking to the road, foreshadows a parting idealized and institutionalized in Indian culture—the embarkation of the renunciate. It was considered the supreme accomplishment for a man, after he had fulfilled himself erotically, financially, and domestically as a householder, to renounce all ties, all love, and become a mendicant for the sake of liberation. After his debate with Śaṅkara, Maṇḍana Miśra renounced worldly life and left his wife in order to wander alone in emulation of Śaṅkara "whose only

wife was himself."[1] Ultimately it was the man's duty to leave
and the woman's to grieve. His religious fulfillment was in
renunciation, hers in devotion.
The parting always comes too soon. Out of love the woman
attempts to delay it, to restrain the man just as matter tries to
captivate spirit. And out of love the man is hesitant, torn, am-
bivalent toward the woman, terrible in her beauty, who inspires
the miserable joy of love. The ambiguous feelings toward the
woman have a paradigm in experience—the infant, nourished
by the mother, experiences warmth and sustenance at her breast
and yet is tyrannized by the need for that nourishment. He is
enslaved by need and desire, thirst and love. When Śaṅkara's
mother, Āryāmbā, was asked by her eight-year-old son for permission to renounce the world, to become a sannyasi, she did
everything in her power to restrain him. "Don't speak to me in
this way. You must marry and become a father and perform the
sacrifices. When you are old you can become a sannyasi. That is
the orthodox way. And how can I live alone? I shall die from
sorrow. . . . How can you leave me, your dear mother? Is your
heart not moved by pity for me in my helpless condition?"[2]
With tears, oaths, and threats the women in Sanskrit love
poetry make the same appeal to their parting lovers. The woman
stands in the man's way. The obstruction makes her religiously
dangerous and erotically compelling. Her sorrow proves the
intensity of her love and tests the strength of the man's resolve:

> "Will you come home to me tomorrow
>   morning, noon or night?"
> She asks her lover in deep sorrow;
> Choked with tears the girl delays
>   the lover whose journey
> Is sure to take one hundred days.[3]

> cloud-splendid skies tear-filled eyes
> now-watching half-speaking somehow
> ". . . if you leave my dearest one . . ."
> robe-clinging earth-clawing and then
> . . . the words turn back. . . .[4]

Words turn back from defining the experience, from describing the event, from depicting the girl, just as they must, according to Śaṅkara, turn back in failure from depiction of the inexpressible reality of *brahman:* "Who can describe That from which words turn back?"[5] The poet merely adumbrates the ineffable unreality of love. The philosopher merely suggests terms which describe not *brahman* but the mind's apprehension of *brahman,* or he differentiates that which is *brahman* from that which is not. In the end, in the search for reality or love, words are lost.

The tears of women are repeatedly juxtaposed with monsoonal rains, "tear-filled eyes" with "cloud-splendid skies," in affirmation of a correspondence between the personal and the natural. Such a correspondence between levels of existence makes magic, ritual, and love possible just as it made it possible for the philosophers to equate *ātman* and *brahman,* the ground of the self and the universal reality. The "pathetic fallacy" does contain the truth of sympathy between the levels of being. The effects of rain and tears are the same just as the cause, an impulse for fertility, is the same. In the woman the impulse expresses itself as love:

> She did not clutch his shirt
> nor reach with clinging arm;
> she did not block the door,
> nor fall at his feet again;
> she did not beg, "please stay."
> Clouds swarmed the dark sky;
> her lover was ready to leave
> but the flood restrained him—
> the waters, her tears.[6]

The poet chooses a word for the lover which means literally "deceitful one"—one of the four types of lovers defined by the rhetoricians. The poet's use of the technical term suggests that the journey is a ploy to camouflage the man's tryst with another woman.

The women attempt to restrain their lovers with threats of death just as Āryāmbā tried to prevent Śaṅkara from becoming a sannyasi by appealing to his pity for her: "I shall die from sorrow . . . and who will be there to perform my funeral rites? How can you leave me? . . ."[7] The female, woman or nature, lover or mother, cannot survive without the male, man or spirit, beloved or child. The impulse for fertility which animates the female, sustaining life on all levels, realizes itself in isolation as an impulse for death.

Departing lovers promise their wives and mistresses that they will return just as Śaṅkara vowed to his mother, frail with age, that he would come home to perform her funeral rites. A young woman, frail with love, makes the same request of her beloved:

> Be patient dearest one.
> 　　　　　　　　*Yes*—patient for all eternity.
> 　　　　　　　　Good-bye . . . good-bye. . . .
> I will come back.
> 　　　　　　　　*Yes*—with gifts of fortune
> 　　　　　　　　　　for your friends.
> Do you want anything?
> 　　　　　　　　*Yes*—a funeral offering
> 　　　　　　　　　　at a sacred pool.[8]

The woman's sorrow is most poignant when she tries to restrain it, to hold back her tears or conceal them with laughter, sarcasm, or silence:

"Don't worry, my lovely one,
you are so very frail; no,
don't worry," I wept,
"for those who part
are sure to meet again."
As I spoke she looked at me;
tears held back,
eyes dull with shame.
She laughed—
I knew she longed for death.[9]

Gushing tears and promises!
Falling at a lover's feet!
With such endearing gestures
Fainthearted ladies try to
Stop their lords from leaving!
Not I! I'm more fortunate!
Well, good luck and good-bye
On the morning of your journey!
(By the way, my dear, once you've gone
you'll no doubt hear that I have taken
certain measures quite appropriate to
love. . . .)[10]

The appropriate measure will be to die. The departure of the
man kills the woman for he is, as lover, the lord god of her living
spirit, her vital breath. Her devotion to him is her religion,
wholly carnal and thoroughly sacred. The passionate and des-
perately loving woman feigns detachment just as the deceitful
lover feigns attachment to a woman he no longer loves. If the
woman is honest she will cry, make promises, fall at her lord's
feet in supplication, but such expressions of love make him anxious to leave and so she pretends to be passionless and conceals
the actual with the act. All women's gestures, the sincere and
the duplicitous alike, arise from the same erotic motive. The
woman clings to the man for dear life:

when
my love
departs
tears
bracelets
friends
all
are gone
with him
my heart
cannot endure
it tries
to follow
why does my life persist
shouldn't it join
the others
who've left
me
here
alone?[11]

In some accounts of the legend of Śaṅkara, the principal wife
of the poet-king Amaru is suspicious that her resurrected lord
is not in fact her husband but a gifted yogi. While Śaṅkara
was occupied with mastering the *Kāmasūtra* through association
with the beautiful women of Amaru's harem, the queen dis-
patched some palace officers to find the unoccupied body of the
holy man and burn it so that the great soul inhabiting her
lover's body would be trapped there for her enjoyment. Several
of Śaṅkara's disciples, having discovered that imperial emis-
saries were searching the countryside for bodies and burning
them, made their way to the palace disguised as musicians. They
sang a song to the king which contained the phrase "you are the
eternal *ātman*," and at once the subtle body of Śaṅkara with-
drew from the gross body of Amaru and returned to the cave
where soldiers were beginning to light the fire to immolate

Śankara's body. Śankara escaped the grasp of sensuality, the clutch of woman, just in time. The sannyasi's hand had already been touched by the flames.[12]

Sexuality is dangerous not because it is in any way inherently wicked or sinful but because it renders the man vulnerable to the woman. The man, trying to leave on a journey or seeking release from the world, is bound by the woman, mother or wife, mistress or *māyā*. "You have seen a woman's full breasts and her navel," a hymn attributed to Śankara solemnly warns. "It is a delusory show of *māyā*—think of it as a mere mass of flesh and fat."[13] The woman's breast is not a source of sustenance as the infant would have it, not a golden urn overflowing with holy water as the poet would have it, but a lump of fat full of death. And ultimately the mistresses of Amaru, all who love, are fated to feel revulsion for the very flesh in which they delight. Śankara preaches renunciation because of the inconstancy of love, the evanescence of pleasure, and the transience of all forms:

> The household asks after one's health
> as long as life remains in the flesh;
> but when breath is gone, body expired,
> the wife will fear her love's corpse.
> We enjoy the pleasures of love
> for the sake of happiness only
> until disease seizes the flesh.
> Adorn yourself with rags for the road.
> Set out upon the path of renunciation
> of the sacred and the profane. Say:
>> I AM NOT
>> YOU ARE NOT
>> THIS WORLD IS NOT
> Then why should you feel any sorrow?[14]

The mother is as dangerous as the mistress: her affection for the man imperils him no less. The woman must let the man go if he is to attain release from the world. Several days after

Āryāmbā had refused to give her son permission to become a
sannyasi, the two of them went to a river to bathe together. As
Śaṅkara stepped into the river a crocodile suddenly took hold of
his leg. The boy cried out to his mother, "Give me permission to
take the sannyasi's vows that I may die a renunciate." The
moment that Āryāmbā gave her consent the crocodile released
Śaṅkara and the boy emerged uninjured from the river. Āryāmbā rushed to her son joyously to guide him home. "No, I cannot
go with you," Śaṅkara explained. "I am a sannyasi now and all
women who give me alms now are my mothers."[15] All women
and none—the sannyasi has no family, no bonds or attachments.

The image of the crocodile expresses Śaṅkara's attitude toward desire and hope, for the objects of sense perception and for
sensual pleasures specifically: "Those who strive for liberation,
beginning their renunciation, trying to cross the ocean of being,
are drowned in the midst of it—the crocodile of hope grabs their
throats and at once they are pulled away. But he who slays the
crocodile named sense pleasure with the sword of dispassion
crosses the waters of existence avoiding all obstacles."[16] The legendary anecdote developed, perhaps, as an illustrative amplification of the philosopher's metaphor. The desire for liberation,
the renunciate's hope, is as dangerous as the desire or hope of
the lover. Śaṅkara, the immaculate child whose heart is set on
renunciation, must wait for his mother's permission; he may not
put his desire for liberation above his duty to obey his parent.
Once Āryāmbā has given her permission it cannot be retracted.
Her son is set free and she has no choice but to endure her soli-
tude, the inevitable loneliness of widows, mothers, and ladies
whose beloveds leave on journeys. The moment of departure,
the freedom from the female, gives a foretaste of the unbound-
ed liberation to come. When the joys and sorrows of living in
relationship to others are renounced a greater joy manifests. Just
as the lover's pursuit of pleasure is full of a miserable passion,
the renunciate's rejection of pleasure is full of a joyous dispassion. The wandering sannyasi, clad only in a scant loincloth,
carrying only a staff and a begging bowl, is traditionally idealized as one who, by having nothing, possesses all:

Blessed indeed are those who wear the loincloth—
Eternally delighting in the sayings of Vedānta,
With only the food given to them as alms,
Roaming with no sorrow in the heart,
Blessed indeed are those who wear the loincloth—
Sleeping only at the foot of a tree,
Eating only from their two hands,
Reviling riches like rags,
Blessed indeed are those who wear the loincloth—
Fulfilled by their own innate joy,
Turning all the senses to complete peace,
Delighting in the happiness of *brahman* day and night,
Blessed indeed are those who wear the loincloth—
Overthrowing the state of the body and mind,
Seeing only the Self within one's self,
Remembering nothing within, without, in between,
Blessed indeed are those who wear the loincloth—
Uttering the sacred syllable of *brahman*,
Thinking "I am *brahman!*"
Living on alms and wandering everywhere,
Blessed indeed are those who wear the loincloth.[17]

Śaṅkara set out upon the road, began a solitary journey
through the world in order to be delivered from the world, a
journey away from home to find the true home deep within
himself. Seated, still, silent, Śaṅkara immersed himself in contemplation of the *ātman*, the changeless aspect of oneself that is
brahman. The hagiographer senses the erotic aspect of the en-
deavor: "As an artless girl, gently urged on by her friends,
enters the bridal chamber and little by little abandons her self-
consciousness and then unites with her lord and then forgets
herself completely, becoming one with him, so did the sage
Śaṅkara, guided by the powers of discrimination as established
in the Vedānta philosophy, enter into himself and little by little
he abandoned his self-consciousness and united with his Lord
and forgot himself, realizing his complete identity with It, the
supreme Self, *ātman, brahman.*"[18] The artless maiden's lord,

her husband or lover, the object of her love, causes misery by his absence and gives joy with his embraces. In sexual union she experiences a suspension of ego-activity, a blissful death, in which two seem to be one. The sannyasi's lord, his chosen deity, is a qualified dimension of an unqualified reality. This object of devotion and meditation causes misery by creating the world and gives joy by pointing the way to the reality which he symbolizes. The adept uses god to get beyond god, to realize himself as It: an infinite continuum of being, awareness, and bliss in which there is no lover-beloved, devotee-deity, subject-object. For the lover, for Amaru and his courtiers and courtesans, there is the inevitable return—that which in a surpassing moment seemed one becomes two, a man and woman, once more. For the renunciate, for Śaṅkara and his disciples, there is the ultimate return to a state which precedes creation—that which seemed two becomes one, *brahman*, once more.

The sannyasi's meditation is an internalization of the Vedic sacrifice in which the empirical self is burned away on an inner altar by the fire of asceticism. The self is sacrificed to the Self, the "I" to the "It." Such enstatic contemplation threatens the gods by depriving them of the offerings which sustain and empower them. Indra, his rainbow weapon ready, comes to the aid of the mythological realm with monsoonal storms to disturb sannyasis and weaken their concentration. "How do these renunciates, full of pride over their understanding of Advaita Vedānta, dare," the god asks, "to cease making the sacrificial offerings to me, the leader of the gods, the tributes which all men owe?"[19] It is not only Śaṅkara's meditation which menaces the gods; his teaching, Advaita Vedānta, is an even greater threat. Śaṅkara is portrayed as the avatar who teaches the illusoriness of the avatars, a man-god who teaches that both men and gods are pale and insubstantial phantoms. He does so out of a detached compassion for the transient beings who are caught in the snare of love and of Love. As the god Śaṅkara (Śiva) destroyed Love (Kāma), the teacher Śaṅkara destroys love *(kāma)*; as the god destroyed the sacrifice of demons, the teacher destroys the sacrifices of men. And so as Śaṅkara sat in meditation, Indra unleashed his torrential assault. Soon the Narmadā river began to flood and the villages on its banks were imperiled. The cries of the people drew Śaṅkara back into the phenomenal realm and he uttered a powerful mantra, an incantation to control the flood, and he gathered the waters in his water jug.[20]

Though the villagers celebrate the triumph of Śaṅkara, it is, in a sense, Indra who has won in that Śaṅkara has been forced to return to the empirical world, the realm of grateful sacrifices. The "It" has been made the "I" once more and *māyā* is reimposed upon *brahman*. This oscillation between the absolute and the relative on the ontological level, or fluctuation between the experience which is the Self and the experience of the self on the psychological level, is mythologically exemplified by Śiva as he vacillates between passivity and activity—between ascetic performances which drain the energy of the universe and dance performances which, like his lovemaking with the goddess and his battles with demons, reenergize the universe. Śaṅkara and Amaru manifest the dyadic phases of the deity. As rain distracts the holy man, it enchants the lover. As rain, sent by a virile god, fecundates the feminine earth, men and women are inspired to lovemaking. Just as sannyasis, who normally wandered, were forced to spend the monsoon season in a single place, courtiers and city men, who normally traveled to conduct business or battle, were kept at home with their women by the rains. The conventional fear of the man on the road is that the rains will come before he returns home, that the season will keep him away from his beloved. And in that separation all the erotic associations generated by the rain will intensify the pain of longing. A man, away from his beloved at night, sings a song of love as the rains come. And the villagers, hearing it, renounce any ideas they may have had about traveling as well as all jealousy and anger—all that might keep them distant from those closest to them:

Clouds, water burdened, groaning,
slowly moved across the night.
A traveler, trembling, grieving,
sang a litany of sorrow.
Those who heard the feeling
could not think of leaving,
of uttering the deadly words.
And with outstretched hands
they said good-bye to fooling pride.[21]

The erotic poem suggests religious attitudes: the traveler suggests a mendicant; the literal night implies the figurative spiritual darkness of the degenerate age; the "litany of sorrow" (literally, the song telling of "the sadness of his own separation"
[*ātma-viyoga-duḥkha*]) suggests a hymn which tells of the exis-
tential unease *(duḥkha)* of nonintegration *(viyoga)* with the Self
(ātman). When people of the world hear it they give up their
egotism and pride. Antipodal modes of experience are momentarily and faintly reconciled through the ambiguity of the poetic
language. The religious permeates the erotic in the poem as
Śaṅkara's spirit permeated the body of Amaru. The same ambiguity pervades all phenomena and all structures—things are
only what they are interpreted to be. In a single form Śaṅkara's
disciples see a saintly philosopher and Amaru's wives see an
amorous poet. The lover is a kind of holy man: his fidelity to his
beloved during his journey is a kind of celibacy and his love song
a kind of devotional hymn.

The song of the lover and the chant of the pilgrim both
inspire seriousness in those who hear it. Both demand gentle-
ness, kindness, an appreciation of the fragility of things. But,
for Amaru, the seriousness must not be taken too seriously or it
becomes bathos. The scene which can be depicted with the amorous mood lends itself to the humorous mood as well:

In a village once a traveler was given refuge from a storm:
He thought of his beloved, so far away, so lovely and so
  warm.
> All night long he sang a sad, sad song,
> A song of separation, sung in lamentation,
> With deep-drawn sighs and tear-filled eyes.
In the morning the villagers said, when he was out of sight,
"That's the last time we'll ever let a traveler spend the
  night!"[22]

The villagers need sleep after their day of labor; the lover needs
the sleeplessness of longing for the beloved, an expression of his
restless dedication to love. Love has elevated him above the natural needs to which the peasants remain subject. Love is an ele-
vation of the natural, procreative urge, the instinct for survival;
it is a transformation of the crude into the refined.

The biological need for release of tension becomes, through
the courtly invention of love, a refined art, entertaining and
moving, amusing and full of meanings the villager cannot
know. Love is a poetic invention by the leisured for their own
use. Love as a cultural institution, as an aesthetic ideal, does not
exist for the peasant. It exists for those who play, not for those
who work. It was the sport of the courtier, the aristocrat, or the
urbane gentleman whose daily routine consisted of adorning
himself and teaching parrots to speak, listening to music and
composing poetry, discussing the arts and indulging in witty
repartee. Courtly love, the pastime of the sophisticated man
about town, the aristocratic *rasika,* was a reconciliation of individual erotic impulses with collective erotic ideals. Poetry was a
medium for the reconciliation. As the gods produced the world
by churning the cosmic ocean for the nectar of immortality, the
poets produced a world with its own aesthetic order by churning
the chaos of actual life to extract the nectar, the *rasa.* This poetic
world, marked by sweetness and elegance, perspicuity and refinement, was the private estate of an intellectual and social
elite.

Religion was no less elite, no less private, than love. Śaṅkara's transcendental religious philosophy was the guarded seizin of a spiritual aristocracy. Only erudite male brahmins seem to have been eligible for initiation into Vedāntic study.[23] The hymns in which Śaṅkara purportedly expresses popular sentiments, ardent devotion to personal gods, clearly postdate him by centuries. Both the hymns and the biographical legends compromise Śaṅkara. The intellectual philosopher and chaste preceptor is popularized into a god and a hero. The hagiographers tell of Śaṅkara's encounter with an untouchable. The man, accompanied by four dogs, stood in the way of the holy man who was going to the river to bathe. Śaṅkara ordered him to get out of his path, to stay away from him. The untouchable responded, "When you, O supreme renunciate, say, 'Get away, get away!' what is it that you wish to go away? Is it one body made of food from another body or is it mind from mind? In the inner reality, there is no difference between a brahmin and an untouchable— is there any difference in the sun which is reflected in the waters of the Ganges and the sun which is reflected in the puddles in the streets where the untouchables live?" At once Śaṅkara fell prostrate before the low-caste man and asked him to be his preceptor with the recitation of a verse:

> I am not what you see
> *I AM*
> the consciousness illuminating
> waking   dreams   deep sleep
> the world witness pervading all
> smallest ant   greatest god
> He is my guru
> untouchable or brahmin
> who has this wisdom[24]

The moment Śaṅkara accepted the pariah as his preceptor, he realized that the man was Śiva in disguise. The dialogue between the brahmin and the untouchable is but a dialogue between two manifestations of Śiva: Śaṅkara and the untouchable are one. One manifestation instructs the other to write commentaries on the Veda, to appoint disciples, and to spread the truth of Vedānta throughout India. One returns to the heavens, the other travels the earth.

The holy man must keep moving, Śaṅkara warned the disciple Padmapāda: "Do not stay too long in any one place. It will create attachments." Śaṅkara explains further that even staying with fellow sannyasis is dangerous: "When you part with them it causes the heart great sorrow, just as it gives joy when you are with them."[25]

The sorrow which the renunciate attempts to overcome by travel is the same sorrow that the lover experiences through travel. In separation, through the journey, lovers share a single pain. Their division is their unity. Separated lovers have impossible hopes and make futile gestures. Love is a noble commitment to senselessness and futility. No character is as absurd or as heroic as the lover. His sentimentality has conviction.

> HE   is separated from   HER
> by many lands, by many
> rivers, mountains, forests
> and yet
> stretching his neck
> rubbing his eyes
> standing on his toes
> straining his eyes
> imagining somehow
> he might see her
> he looks again in her direction[26]

To love is to wait, to be anxious and feel the ache of time. Ceaselessly lovers combat time, seek refuge from it in desperate embraces, seek to contract it in separation and expand it in union. Time is personified in Indian mythology as Yama, the gatherer of men. His flesh is green and his robes blood red. He carries a noose in one hand and a club in the other. The eyes of Time glow in the darkness of death. Yama's sister, Yamī, loved

her brother passionately and mourned so deeply for him when
he was gone that the gods created night to console her, a darkness in which she could hide her grief. Women longing for their
traveling lovers weep in the night. They hope, imagine, remem-
ber, tremble, wait:

> She watched the road by which her lover would come,
> Looked as far as the eye could see: it was desolate.
> As dusk passed into spreading night she walked alone
>   toward home. . . .
> >   With a sudden turn—
> >   Maybe he's coming—
> >   She looked for him
> >   Once more.[27]

>   I imagine a young girl weeping:
> In a garden in a courtyard
>   she clutches clustered blossoms,
> Bouquets brilliant with buzzing bees
>   lusting for oozing saps and mango pollen;
> Covering herself, sighing, breasts shuddering,
>   she holds back the cries and her throat
> Is filled with tremors.[28]

> >   tears from eyes that
> >   watched the road fell
> >   upon her breasts
> >   the surface pale
> >   as if white-hot from
> >   fires of love
> >   flames of separation:
> >   *tssss* . . . .
> >   *tssss* . . . .
> >   *tssss* . . . .
> >   . . . . .droplets
> >   on a scorching iron[29]

A young girl separated from her lover resorts to the conventionally prescribed remedies for the burning sorrow of love: "a garland, a wet compress, moist sandal paste, lotus petals, seeking refuge in Himalayan breezes dispersing their snowy mists. . . ." Yet since these antidotes, reminding the girl of her traveling lover, become the very "kindling . . . how shall the fire of love ever be extinguished?"[30] The word the poet uses for the extinction of the fire, *nirvāṇa*, creates an ambiguity. The profane, erotic activity of the girl parodies the sacred, ascetic activity of the renunciate who, in emulation of Śiva, performs mountain penances for the sake of *nirvāṇa*, the extinction of the fire of rebirth. A single road leads in two opposite directions.

Nirvāṇa is traditionally explained with the metaphor of putting out a lamp, of calming it, and one's self. By means of restraint the renunciate puts out the lamp and frees himself from illusions; by means of an illusion a loving woman puts out the lamp and frees herself from restraints when her lover returns from his journey:

> Anxious with fantasies by the ten million,
> She waited until her dear lover returned;
> She took him at once to her love pavilion
> Where, while passion and a lamplight burned,
> Inconsiderate friends were all hanging about;
> So she swatted a bug in a frightened fashion
> With her shawl, a pretense; the lamp went out—
> Out with the light, but not with the passion![31]

The return home is comic relief. Playful frivolity balances the anxious melancholy of separation. Lovers are as ludicrous as they are noble. Two lovers just reunited after a journey are so anxious to make love that their very excitement prevents enjoyment:

> The long separated, weakened lovers,
>   once they were reunited,
> Greeted—at once the world seemed new—
>   O they were excited!
> The day passed: they talked and talked
>   till they grew hoarse—
> They spent more time on talk than on
>   the other sort of intercourse.[32]

Some reunions are made playful so that the sorrow of love does not eclipse its mirth; others are made tender so that mirth does not overwhelm love's deepest feelings:

> Not blue lotuses but her eyes
> are the garlands at the doorway;
> her smiles are the offerings,
> not jasmine, not nutmeg,
> not any other flower;
> the vessels of libation
> are not pitchers, but her
> breasts full and wet—
> Auspicious gestures, carnal benedictions
> for the arrival of the slender lady's lord.[33]

Again Amaru uses religious language, but it is the vocabulary of devotion and not of asceticism. In devotion the erotic and the religious merge. The lady is as devoted to her lord in the home as the priest is devoted to the Lord in the temple: the lover is as devoted to his lady as the devotee is enamoured with the goddess. It is in recollection that the sacred and profane impulses overlap. In the erotic tradition "remembrance" is a synonym for "love." It is the amorous activity of separated lovers, the emotional process which enables lovers to experience union in separation and to take delight in their misery:

> Who would not remember her face?
> When away: melancholy
> pale & drawn
> curls loose
> languid
> Upon return: lovely bright
> proud & eager
> for love . . .
> With all my care I kissed her face.[34]

In the religious tradition the "remembered texts" refer to the Veda and "remembrance" is a synonym for "devotion." The recollective activity of the votary is the emotional process which enables the devotee to experience the transcendent in the immanent. As a religious practice remembrance is a bringing to mind of the deity's qualities, a singing of praise. Devotional hymns attributed to Śaṅkara display remembrance of the goddess's face, recollection as ardent as Amaru's: "Your face," the petitioner sings, "shames the lotus, surpasses it in beauty, surrounded as it is by young bees—your naturally curling tresses!"[35] Devotional recollection and amorous remembrance are both forms of meditation, modes for the inner experience of outer realities. The former is a prelude to reintegration, the latter to reunion.

Immersed in meditation Śaṅkara had a vision of his mother—she was dying. Remembering his vow to return to perform her funeral obsequies, he transported himself with his yogic powers to her side and "he who was firm in nonattachment became tenderhearted on seeing his mother."[36] Śaṅkara tried to soothe his dying mother with Vedāntic instruction, with explanations that old age and death are but illusions, that the one reality, *brahman,* is ageless, deathless, beyond all mutability and sorrow. His mother explained that she could find no consolation in the philosophical unction, no solace in abstract ideas about an impersonal and unqualified godhead. She asked him to enumerate the qualities of god and help her recollect the beauty of a compassionate deity. At once Śaṅkara began to sing a hymn to Śiva:

> Trident-bearing slayer of Love . . .
> Your throat is blue and
> Your emblem is the bull;
> Five-headed Lord of the Universe,
> The thousand-headed serpent
> Is your bracelet . . . and
> You rule the cremation ground. . . .
> Slayer of Love, Lord of Śakti,
> Save us from the abyss of sorrow,
> This world of birth and death.[37]

Śaṅkara sang so perfectly that his mother could see the god standing before her. This vivid vision of the deity, his ashen body, his serpent-encircled arms, his fiery trident, so terrified her that Śaṅkara began to sing a hymn in praise of Viṣṇu, a hymn which gave Āryāmbā a more benign vision of a gentler aspect of *brahman:*

> I praise the lotus-foot of Beauty's Lord,
> Its honey, a divine river,
> Its fragrance and taste,
> Being & Awareness & Joy—
> It dispels the afflictions,
> The terrors of this world. . . .
> You whose mouth is a beautiful lotus,
> You who churned the cosmic ocean, . . .
> Dispel my vast terror![38]

Śaṅkara's mother died with Viṣṇu standing beautiful before her and she was absorbed, according to the hagiographers, into the personal god, delivered from this dreadful round of rebirth to take her place in Viṣṇu's heaven.

Since sannyasis, having renounced all domestic ties, are not permitted to perform family rites, Śaṅkara asked his mother's neighbors to prepare the cremation. They refused to assist him and so he cursed them angrily and performed the rites himself. The fires of death, the crematory flames, burned as fires of love, just as the fires of love, the flames of human attachment, burn as fires of death. Śaṅkara's last tie to the world was gone. He set out once more upon the road to speak of *brahman* and to preach the way of renunciation.

. . . the water soft,
Without forcing or strength,
Where that it falleth oft
Hard stones doth pierce at length.

. . . the wind
My fired mind
Doth still inflame,
And she unkind,
That did me bind,
Doth turn it all to game.

SIR THOMAS WYATT

CHAPTER FOUR

Confrontations

ŚAṄKARA'S PARENTS, according to tradition, had been unable to
have a child. They prayed to Śiva, made offerings, and performed rigorous austerities. One night as they slept their dreams
merged into a single vision of the Great Lord, who promised
that he would grant their wish and give them a son, but he
demanded that they make a choice: "Either you may have a
child who will live long but will be in no way remarkable, or you
may have a child who will be completely wise and virtuous but
will live only a short time." Āryāmbā and her husband, Śiva-
guru, chose the remarkable, short-lived child. Āryāmbā's body
became radiant, glowing with the glory of Śaṅkara, the avatar of
Śiva.[1] Śaṅkara was destined by their choice to die at the age of
eight (the age when the crocodile attacked him in the river), but
when his mother gave him permission to become a sannyasi, the
figurative rebirth of initiation became literal and Śaṅkara was
given eight more years of life.

One day the young philosopher, whose sixteenth year was drawing to a close, was sitting in meditation on the banks of the Ganges when a priest appeared before him. The man began to question Śaṅkara on the meaning of the *Brahmasūtras* and to engage the young renunciate in debate over the essential teachings of Vedānta. As the two argued, Śaṅkara's disciple Padmapāda realized that it was not a priest sitting with his teacher—it was Vyāsa, the legendary "arranger" of the Veda, the supposed author of the *Mahābhārata,* the *Purāṇas,* and the *Brahmasūtras.* As Śaṅkara was a descent of Śiva, Vyāsa was a descent of Viṣṇu. The mythological antipathy between the gods, and its resolution, was acted out on earth in the debate between the two men. "What must a disciple do," Padmapāda cried out, "when Śaṅkara and Vyāsa do not agree, when Śiva and Viṣṇu are at odds?" Realizing the identity of his opponent, Śaṅkara fell in obeisance at his feet. Vyāsa then bowed to Śaṅkara and explained to Padmapāda that there is no difference between Viṣṇu and Śiva: he was only pretending to disagree with Śaṅkara in order to elicit the subtleties of his discourse on Vedānta and thus gain access to the depths of his understanding. Satisfied with the perfection of Śaṅkara's knowledge, Vyāsa granted him another lifetime, sixteen more years, to perform a "tour of victory" throughout India. His mission was to unite all the sects, the Śaivas, Vaiṣṇavas, and Śāktas, and all subsects and cults, to inspire them to realize that their chosen deities were but mere reflections of the one truth, *brahman,* mere guises hiding the one reality. He was to persuade the Buddhists and Jains to give up their heretical teachings and practices and return to the truth of the Veda; by showing the adherents of all philosophical schools their errors, he was to persuade them to assent to the supremacy of Advaita Vedānta. Retrospectively Śaṅkara is esteemed as a champion of national solidarity. He is seen not only as a religious and intellectual conciliator but as a proponent of political and social unity as well.[2]

As Vyāsa disagreed with Śaṅkara in order to draw out his wis-

dom and test his insights, the women in Amaru's poetry often
disagree with their lovers, even show anger and jealousy, in
order to test the depth and intensity of the lover's passion. In
confrontation anger can be a pretext or it can be genuine. In
either case, like the propriety of elders or the obligation of
travel, the lovers' quarrel provides the crucial separation which
inspires ardent longing for union. Each union inspires hopes for
persistence, the taste of pleasure which makes the suffering of
separation sweet. Each painful separation is full of pleasurable
intimations of union. Amaru's collection charts a movement of
lovers, together and apart. There is an erotic pattern: union,
separation, reunion, reseparation—the pattern is circular and
self-contained.

According to the *Kāmasūtra* men disdain women who make
themselves too readily available, who are too easily conquered or
too willing to forgive. A loving woman must put up a fight
against a man, for men, knowing there is nothing noble in van-
quishing a weak enemy, seek a good match in the battle of love.
The handbook of sexual science explains that the offended lady
should display her anger by shaking her head and crying, by
pounding her chest and tearing off her ornaments, by striking
and kicking her beloved. All the while the gentleman, remaining cool and detached, should try to placate her with flatteries
and gestures of obeisance. The text warns that when he falls at
her feet she should begin to relent.[3]

Amaru, like most court poets, illustrated the ideals established in the treatises. The woman cultivates the arts of sulking
and anger; the man cultivates the arts of seduction and pacifica-
tion. The relationship between them is built upon their mastery
of these subtle, complementary arts. The poet describes "the
eye of a sulking woman—it is skilled in assuming a variety of
forms when her lover is guilty":

it looks, anxious,
    when he's far away;
it turns, angry,
    when he tries to stay;
it opens, wide,
    when he starts to speak;
it reddens, bright,
    when he's cheek-to-cheek;
it bends its brow, a creeper,
    when he tugs upon her gown;
it fills at once with tears
    when, repentant, he bows down.[4]

The zeugmatic construction of this poem, the use of multiple verbs and adjectives with the single noun (a common rhetorical figure in the Amaru collection), is a poetic, microcosmic expression of the larger, philosophical notion of the empirical universe as a multiple, fluctuating manifestation of a unitary principle. The technical term in Vedānta for this "appearance of things" is *prapañca,* a word used by the poet in this stanza. The goal of the philosopher is the "extinction of the appearance." Vedānta explains "appearance" as the venturing out of the mind through the senses to an object; sense perception is a modification of the mind as it assumes the manifold forms it beholds. The philosopher endeavors to withdraw the senses, to pull them back as a tortoise pulls its head and legs into its shell. He must, therefore, reject love because by its very nature love affirms the senses and urges the mind to make the venture. The lady's mind reaches out through her eye toward the beloved to assimilate him. The lover is transformed by the beloved through perception.

While the philosopher might be able to affirm the value of devotional love, in either its religious or domestic expressions, as a step toward renunciation in that it concentrates the mind on the one, passionate love by its very nature must be condemned as ignorance, as a deadly, binding fire, for in passion the senses delight in the many. For the poet domestic affection is merely an acceptable condition setting the scene for illicit love.

Amaru's poems evince the aristocratic attitudes and leisured sensibilities of a polygamous society where promiscuity was a formalized masculine virtue. The clever rake, motivated by a rapacious and yet refined appetite for a multiplicity of women, became a conventional and idealized figure. His faithlessness expresses both detachment, a religious ideal, and bravery, a heroic ideal. His ability to lie guiltlessly and cheat remorselessly shows a capacity to revel in passion without attachment to its particular objects, to take pleasure in love without being consumed by it. According to the hagiographers Śaṅkara could sing hymns to many gods and worship at their shrines, recognizing them all as transient manifestations of *brahman*. Likewise the roguish lover adores many women and yet seems detached from any particular woman. He is devoted to the ideal—the beauty and the love, the *rasa*—they embody. Inconstancy becomes a defense against the power of the individual woman:

> On a single couch he saw his ladies
> (not just one, but two);
> The rogue crept up behind them
> (he knew just what to do):
> One lady's eyes he covered up
> (as if to play "Guess Who?");
> He turned to kiss the other one
> (she blushed, a merry hue);
> But she held back her laughter
> (and the other never knew)![5]

The erotic ingenuity and sexual virtuosity requisite for faithlessness are godlike virtues—Kṛṣṇa desired and made love to all the beautiful milkmaids of Vraja and tormented them with delightful jealousy. All were faithful to him. He was faithful to none. The hero, whether in love, war, or religious sacrifice, is unattached to the rewards of action.

> As you embraced me
> your arms loosened
> suddenly when
> you heard the ringing
> girdle jewels jingling
> as another lady moved.
> Cheat! I can't even
> turn to my friend—
> she doesn't care—
> dazed by poison:
>   your buttery words,
>   your honeyed lies.[6]

The devoted woman anxiously awaiting her lover often greets
a man marked with bites, scratches, imprints of another lady's
cosmetics, semaphores of infidelity. The very ornaments which
on a lady inspire love—a bracelet on her arm, mascara on her
eyes, betel on her lips, lac on her feet and hands—inspire anger
or sadness when they appear on a man returning home from
lovemaking:

> In the morning:
>   the armlet's imprint was on his neck,
>   the black mascara was on his face,
>   the red betel stain was on his eyelids,
>   the mark of lac was on his forehead—
> For a long while she looked at her beloved's
>   adornments, incitements to anger, and then
> The young girl sighed into a lotus,
>   the flower with which she had been playing.[7]

Sometimes the hero attempts to conceal the marks; sometimes
he wears them proudly like decorations for heroism in battle.
The marks of teeth, nails, and cosmetics, cherished souvenirs of
love, would reveal to the learned *rasika* the details of the lovemaking that had transpired. The cleverness of the lover standing

marked before his lady (and the cleverness of the poet who has
chosen to write a poem using the motif) is tested:

> Once upon a time a rogue,
>   a very clever rake,
> Appeared before his lady
>   having made a big mistake:
> Alas, forgotten were the marks
>   on his naked chest,
> Unguent stains imprinted there
>   from another's breast!
> Hoping to conceal them,
>   he fell at his lady's feet.
> Too late! Too bad! Egad! She saw!
>   She started to retreat.
> So he stood up with open arms,
>   "Come, show me what you mean."
> When she came close he grabbed her—
>   then his chest was clean,
> For as she rubbed against him
>   the marks were all erased;
> And as he hugged and squeezed her,
>   clinging to her waist,
> His sins were all forgotten
>   In that joyous kiss.
> [The moral of the story is
>   *amo et fac quod vis!*][8]

The ingenuity of the lover's deceits delights the beloved. To
make his beloved forgive him for his transgressions, the rogue
uses the same seductive cunning he used to make the transgressions. His roguishness is his appeal, his lusty infidelity a virtue,
the fulfillment of an ideal.

> My lover was unfaithful,
>   I kicked him out the door;
> But he came back at dusk, yes,
>   back to me once more.
> I did not know that it was he,
>   how could I?—after all—
> He wore my best friend's sari,
>   he even wore her shawl.
> I thought that he was she
>   when she was he cross-dressed,
> So I felt free to speak my mind—
>   secrets were confessed:
> "I want to have a tryst with him,
>   can it be arranged?"
> "That's difficult," he said to me,
>   but then his voice was changed
> As he roared out with laughter
>   and took me in his arms.
> [I knew at once that it was *he*,
>   *she* didn't have such charms!]⁹

The rogue takes on the guise of the girlfriend, as Vyāsa took on the guise of the priest, for the sake of reconciliation. Whether it is a conflict between lovers, teachers, or gods, a resolution can be achieved through mimesis. The notion of a universe as mere appearance, of activity as mere mimicry, establishes the conflict between passion and renunciation and yet the same notion resolves it: the conflict is not real. That is the lesson which Vyāsa taught Padmapāda.

Padmapāda is said to have been the first of Śaṅkara's disciples —he came to the teacher yearning for instruction, yearning for liberation, professing his disdain not only for the pleasures of this world but for all the pleasures of all the heavens as well. As Śaṅkara is the perfect teacher, Padmapāda is represented as the perfect and most chaste disciple. It is he who argues with his master against entering Amaru's body to learn of love. Because

he is a human being and not an avatar, he must be more faithful
to the renunciatory path taught by Śaṅkara than Śaṅkara himself. Like women in the harem, women who are depicted in
the poetry displaying their pique over the attention their lover
shows another favorite, Śaṅkara's disciples display their pride,
jealous over the attention Śaṅkara pays to Padmapāda. In order
to demonstrate to the others Padmapāda's superiority he called
out from across the Ganges to the chaste student. Immediately,
without thinking, the devoted disciple ran across the river and
lotuses sprang up under Padmapāda's feet to support him on
the water.[10] Śaṅkara embraced him. The guru is to his students
as the lover is to his women—he may care for many, they may
love only one.

Jealous pride is also said to be the reason why many of the
proponents of non-Vedāntic schools wished to debate Śaṅkara.
Philosophical debate is an intellectual form of the same confrontation, the same impulse toward conflict resolution, which
manifests erotically in the arguments of lovers. Both are agonis-
tic forms of seduction; both are battles of wit demanding dialec-
tical virtuosity. In debate the philosophers display linguistic
skills and play upon the multiple meanings of words to con-
found their opponents. The dialogue between Maṇḍana Miśra
and Śaṅkara operates on various levels which are held together
through the ambiguities of language. When Maṇḍana Miśra
pauses incorrectly between words, for example, Śaṅkara rather
than responding to the content of Maṇḍana's speech, chides his
opponent for making the grammatical error of "breach of caesura" *(yati-bhaṅga)*. Since the word *yati,* meaning "caesura"
(from √*yam,* "to pause"), can also mean "a renunciate" (from
√ *yat,* "to strive"), Maṇḍana can reply, "It was my intention to
commit *yati-bhaṅga,* the defeat of a renunciate!" But, due to
the ambiguity of Sanskrit compounds, Śaṅkara can throw the
phrase back at him once again: "Well you have suffered *yati-
bhaṅga,* defeat *by* a renunciate!"[11]

Lovers, moving from one semantic level to another, manipu-

late language in the same way. Loveplay demands wordplay and
wordplay is foreplay. In order to seduce his beloved, a lover uses
abstract nouns correctly in such a way that embraces become,
ironically, the logical way for the beloved to express her anger.
The lover's linguistic skill gives his absurd request logical consis-
tency:

> Since you feel only anger, then
>   let anger be your mate.
> But now, let's settle love's account,
>   it really cannot wait:
> Remember the embraces I gave you
>   before we had this row?
> With interest you must give them back,
>   all of them, right now.[12]

There are many weapons in the lover's arsenal of seduction,
many maneuvers and strategies to inveigle an angry woman.
The poet creates new configurations of strategy and counter-
strategy to give the conventional situation a poetic vitality. In
the elaborate game of courtship there is a basic pattern with
seemingly endless variations: the man is unfaithful to his lady
(though he loves her) which makes her angrily jealous which
makes him try to seduce her which makes her repulse him
(though she loves him) which makes him fall at her feet which
makes her pull away which makes him threaten to leave which
makes her weep forgivingly which makes him weak which . . .
and so it goes until they make love. The cycle, like the round of
existence itself, is completed and the circular game of union-
separation-reunion, like the cosmic play of birth-death-rebirth,
begins again and again and again.

This erotic game, this war game, is fought with alternating
parries and thrusts of sincerity and duplicity, truthfulness and
lies. It is hard to tell one from the other in that courtship entails
endless reversals. Truthfulness becomes a kind of lie, a seductive

pose; sincerity is diplomacy and honesty an enticement. The game, as described by the poet, seems to be played with full consciousness that it is a game and yet with the understanding that it cannot be won unless it is played in earnest. The play must be performed as if it were real. Śaṅkara speaks and acts within the illusion as if the illusion were real. This "as-if-real-ness" of things is the most substantial quality in the Vedāntic or erotic vision of the universe.

A lady playfully shows anger in order to initiate the game, to perpetuate the cycle, and she is necessarily disappointed if her lover cannot rise to the occasion in passionate reconciliation:

> In bed together
> He mentions the name of another lady,
>   her rival, and at once
> She turns away, feelings hurt and angry
>   despite his desperate flattery;
> He becomes silent, slighted by his lady,
>   the innocent girl;
> She turns back to check on him—
> "He can't be tired . . . *can he?*"[13]

When the lover mentions a rival lady's name in the presence of his beloved, a frequently repeated motif, it suggests an interchangeability of women as objects of seduction and enjoyment. It is not so much the objects as it is the seduction itself that brings pleasure. In the religious dimension as well, the objects of devotion are secondary—hymns to Śiva, Viṣṇu, and the goddess are attributed to Śaṅkara with the implicit understanding that it does not matter which manifestation of the sacred is addressed and adored. *Brahman* is not a divinity but divinity itself: the nameless, formless divinity of all the divinities. The poet depicts love, the *rasa,* rather than lovers. He describes Woman, the beauty of all beauties, rather than specific beautiful women. He names no names, distinguishes no forms. Each woman simply personifies the ideal—she is as splendid as a lotus; her thick black hair curls around her moonlike face; her lower lip is succulent red and her brows are curved like a creeper; her waist is thin, her thighs firm, her breasts round and full. The legendary wives of Amaru, each indistinguishable from the other, seem to merge into one exquisite type. The devotional panegyrics to the goddess which are ascribed to Śaṅkara portray her in the same terms; she looks the same. All the goddesses, the consorts of all the gods, merge in her.[14] Woman and the goddess are the terrestrial and heavenly vessels for an abstract ideal; they provide access to the transcendental. It is, then, not surprising that one of Amaru's lovers confuses not only his mistresses' names but their forms as well:

> In the presence of the girl I love
>   I made a big mistake:
> I said another lady's name;
>   my heart began to quake.
> I looked down, embarrassed,
>   and scribbled on the ground:
> There in random doodles
>   a portrait could be found—
> not a picture of my girl
>   but the other lady's face!
> Yes, her again! O awful curse!
>   O terrible disgrace!
> Crying, blushing, flush with anger,
>   her cheeks a burning red,
> She put a foot—O deadly weapon—
>   upon my lowered head.[15]

The confusion of names and forms, the conventional erotic motif, parodies a philosophical theme—in the Vedānta system "name-and-form" is a technical term for a source of ontological ignorance. The transient, relative, empirical world, *māyā*, is but "name-and-form"—the mere names and forms give an impression to the ignorant of an actual and substantial multiplicity. The one true self, *ātman,* is differentiated into selves and the one true reality, *brahman,* is differentiated into things, merely on the basis of different names and forms. The true oneness, the one trueness, according to Śaṅkara, has nothing to do with, is utterly untouched by, "name-and-form." "The entire universe," he explains, "which out of ignorance is perceived to have many forms is only *brahman.* . . . A pot made of clay is not different than clay."[16] A pot is neither the shape of the pot nor the name "pot"; it is the clay which precedes it, the clay which will persist when the pot is broken, the pieces scattered. Individuals appear and disappear, come and go; *brahman,* the purest ideal, endures forever as it has always been.

The women in Amaru's collection embody ideals of physical beauty. The men embody social ideals, perfections of character: cleverness, daring, sportiveness, nobility, honor. The men are without physique or physiognomy—they are pure word and gesture. The lovers in the poetry, like all beings in the universe described by Śaṅkara, are fleeting shadows. Though they touch, they are intangible.

In both the religious and the secular traditions, the abstract ideal is valued for its presumed universality and eternal continuity. Beyond "name-and-form" the philosopher apprehends the transcendental *brahman* and the poet apprehends the transcendental *rasa.* Both confront the universal where the ignorant see only the specific. The particular is but a dim reflection of the ideal. "Seeing the reflection of the sun mirrored in the water in a pot," Śaṅkara explains, "the fool thinks it is the sun."[17] Amaru plays upon this traditional philosophical metaphor:

> Cool reflections in the wine
> sulking women drank the moon.
> It penetrated anger's mine,
> their hearts, and very soon
> the women's hearts began to shine.[18]

As wine can inspire forgiveness, it can also cause fresh anger:

> *Memoria in aeterna:*
> mead drunken girl
> didn't know
> what she was doing
> noticing the nailmark
> the wound
> she had inflicted
> was jealous
> tried to leave
> I tugged
> her robe's hem
> "where are you going?"
> she turned
> faced me
> tearful eyes
> trembling lips
> anger
> "let go of me
> let go . . ."[19]

Any cause can engender antithetical effects. A vision of the world as a tedious and unreal round of rebirth and redeath can inspire either passion or renunciation in equal measure. Amaru and Śaṅkara represent polarized reactions to the same world. They run in opposite directions from the same center. The lover expresses outwardly, in his passionate behavior, the inner life of the renunciate, the desperate desire which fuels his renunciation. The renunciate expresses outwardly, in his dispassionate behavior, the inner life of the lover, the desperate detachment which creates the need for love. They are paradoxical.

Lovers prove the paradox and perversity of love continuously. The self-contradictory nature of erotic impulse provides the underlying humor of Amaru's poems as well as their underlying poignancy. Men are faithless to the women they love and women are angry with the men they love. Angry women reject their lovers only to the degree to which they are attracted to them. It does not matter who inflicted the wound—the drunken girl *must* display pique. The greater the love, the greater the anger and the more vehement the rejection of the beloved. And yet the greater the love, the more difficult it will be to display that greater anger and to repulse the faithless rogue. In love, as in renunciation, the more one desires not to desire, the less successful one is:

> I BEND MY BROW IN ANGER
> *and yet,* all the while
> my eyes look at him
> with longing;
> I REFUSE TO SPEAK
> *and yet,* all the while
> I can hardly keep
> from smiling;
> MY MIND IS FIRM
> *and yet,* all the while
> my flesh bristles
> with delight;
> MY ANGER WOULD SUCCEED
> *if only* my lover
> were nowhere
> to be seen.[20]

> face to face
> with him
> i bowed my head
> glanced at his feet

> though ears were eager
> anxious and curious
> to hear his voice
> i covered them

with my hands
i hid
sweating cheeks
the bristling of delight

but what could i do
my friends
when the seams of my bodice
split in a hundred places?[21]

LET MY HEART BREAK!	impetuously she speaks
LET LOVE DESTROY ME!	with swelling pride
I DON'T NEED HIM!	but anxiously she watches
A LOVER WHOSE LOVE	the path by which
IS SO INCONSTANT!	he might come to her.[22]

Despite the difficulties of showing anger the woman must somehow make the effort so that the man can display his virtuosity as a seducer. He may try to dominate her or submit to her, to be aggressive or regressive; he may reprimand her like a stern father or beg forgiveness like a naughty child; he may threaten to leave her, renouncing all pleasure like an ascetic, or he may fall at her feet like a devotee performing obeisance before the goddess in whom he finds all delight:

"Look at me and speak to me please;
I'm at your feet on my hands and my knees.
You've never been this angry before. . . ."
She turned; she wept; she spoke no more.[23]

As in her hands she held the moon,
her face, and as anger softened,
and when there could be no more strategies
and my only hope, my only refuge,
was to fall down in supplication
then she forgave me with her tears,
    tears her eyelids had held back
    tears which fell upon her breast.[24]

The faithless lover used the same words and gestures before his beloved as those which the faithful votary chants and displays before the goddess. Seduction is the goal of both lover and holy man and of their professional equivalents, the poet and the priest. The lover flatters his beloved; the poet praises the beauty of woman; the devotee and the priest sing hymns to the divinity, sacred encomia, holy flattery. Praise is a hopeful and devout expression of love, whether carnal or chaste.

A popular South India legend tells that the goddess went on a rampage in Kāñcī, dancing madly, crushing buildings beneath her feet, shaking the earth, threatening to destroy the temples to the other deities. Like the angry woman of poetry, she reviled those who fell at her feet trying to appease the jealousy which their attention to other gods had engendered. But Śaṅkara, according to the legend, like the clever lover, had the skill and seductive power to assuage her cosmic pique. He saved the sacred city of Kāñcī by singing an ardent hymn to the goddess and by performing a rite of prayerful homage, the religious equivalent of the amorous entreaty which Amaru's lovers make before their ladies. The wrathful goddess was transformed by Śaṅkara into Kāmākṣī: "She with the Eyes of Love." Śaṅkara consecrated an image of her in order to establish her presence in this benign form and he installed before it a geometrical image to be contemplated by devotees. The mystical diagram, formed of interlocking triangles, represented the perfect harmonization of male and female, the complete reconciliation of god and goddess.

Śaṅkara's hymn was successful in subduing the goddess where the obeisances of others had failed, the storyteller says, because his hymn was based upon the precepts of Vedānta. The philosopher's song revealed to the goddess that all deities are but aspects of the unified reality of *brahman;* thus he who worships Śiva or Viṣṇu worships the goddess unknowingly. As the amorous lady displays her anger in order to be seduced, so the goddess is ferocious in order to be propitiated. As jealousy is a necessary extension of love, so the destructive aspect of the deity is an inherent extension of divine grace and beneficence.

The ferocious aspect of the goddess in her hideous form, eyes blazing like coals, mouth frothing with blood, is worshiped with propitiation; the gentle aspect of the goddess in her lovely form, eyes like lotuses, mouth dripping with nectar, is worshiped with adoration. Both forms converge in the goddess invoked by Amaru, the goddess who slew the buffalo-headed demon. The essential female ambivalence expressed in the paradoxical mythology of the goddess persists on every level of manifestation. As nature the feminine principle encompasses both the degenerative and regenerative forces, birth and death, abundance and famine. As the mother she simultaneously protects and overwhelms, alternately nourishes and denies. As the lady of erotic poetry she is tender and harsh, supple and fierce, alluring and forbidding, full of love and anger. The anger of women is depicted as an allurement, an expression of love. "Long live the ardent love of the slender girl," the poet sings," even her fury is displayed with charm!"[25] The two aspects of the feminine are inextricably intermeshed. Inner and outer contradict each other. Anger seduces the man, invites him to seduce the woman:

> Cautiously he asked her friends one night,
> "Why does she sleep dressed in her clothes?
> Why is her girdle still buckled so tight?"
> "He won't let me sleep!" She angrily said
> and then rolling over as if trying to doze
> she made room for her lover to join her in bed.[26]

The devotees of the ferocious incarnations of the goddess see her hideous form as beautiful and experience her terrible fury as bliss; just so the lover delights in his lady's anger as something divine:

> Brow-bending, finger-shaking and lip-biting
> with lowered eyes the offended lady's fighting—
> "Don't! Stop it! Cheat!" the angry lady hisses
> but there's divine nectar in her angry kisses—
> How stupid of the gods to have churned the ocean
> to come up with immortality's ambrosial potion![27]

To attain the nectar of immortality the gods churn the cosmic ocean, lovers kiss their angry mistresses, and renunciates contemplate the Self:

> abstaining from ceremonial rites,
> he attains the nectar, Immortality,
> who worships at the holy place—
> his own Self:
>> It is pure; It is eternal joy,
>> dispelling cold and heat;
>> It is everywhere, all pervading.[28]

For Śaṅkara the pleasure of love is a source of pain; for Amaru the pain of love is a source of pleasure. Kicking, biting, scratching, squeezing, a lady expresses the passion of both her desire and her anger. Punishment becomes a reward; to repulse is to entice:

> A man who is kicked by a lady
> for his transgressions in love,
> struck by the painted foot,
> jewelled, delicate, fresh sprout,
> dedicated to a drunken love—
> he's a marked man,
> marked by the Lord,
> the god who is Love.[29]

> She wrapped her arm around him,
> a shackle and yet a tendril,
> sweet and restless;

> She pulled him toward the bedroom,
>   accused him in front of friends—
>   soft, faltering words—"he's done it again!"
> She wept and struck her lucky lover;
>   denying it all,
>   he laughed.[30]

Anger is an erotic divertissement. Amiability in the woman, like constancy in the man, engenders complacency. The most callous woman is she who neither scolds her lover nor breaks down in tears, she whose passion is not play. A lady's calm passivity is devastating: not to show anger belies a greater, more real anger. The cruelest cruelty is in not being cruel:

> Rising to greet him
> she stopped him from joining her on the bed;
>   Fetching betel for him to chew
> she fended off impetuous embraces;
>   Keeping servants close at hand
> she made sure he could not say he loved her;
>   And so by being polite
> the clever lady vented her anger on her lord.[31]

> she did not
> bar the door
> nor turn away
> nor speak
> harsh words
> of anger
>
> she just looked
> straight at him
> as if he were
> no different than
> any other man[32]

There is nothing the man can do. The woman must relent. Just
as she must show anger as an expression of love, she must
renounce that anger as a cause of separation at the appropriate
time that the anger may attain its end—reconciliation with the
beloved. Similarly, just as the sannyasi must feel love for his
spiritual preceptor and desire for liberation he must renounce
love and desire at the appropriate time that they may attain
their end—reintegration with the absolute. Loving devotion
may lead to heaven, but only renunciatory knowledge of *brahman* leads to liberation. The former, Śaṅkara taught, is valued
only as a step to the latter.[33]

Women who do not relent, who too vehemently sustain their
anger, live loveless in regret:

> I ignored my lover when he fell down in supplication and
> now
> my lover's face is no more in sight
> and my mouth is scorched with sighs;
> no sleep, I weep both day and night
> and my heart plucked, uprooted, dies. . . .
> What good was there, my friends, in showing anger toward
> my lover?[34]

> when I said "go away"
> it was just a whim;
> he refused to stay;
> now I long for him.[35]

> Anxious, distraught, silent,
> He begged forgiveness at her feet
> and she would have none of it
> and so now he turns away . . .
> she stops him, stares awhile,
> eyes bashful, languid, tearful,
> and her breast trembles with sighs
> and she hopes . . . for life.[36]

Anger recoils on itself and strikes its subject rather than its object. This motif occurs in the hagiographical accounts of Śaṅkara. A tantric adept, a skull-bearing Kāpālika named Krakaca who worshiped and emulated the fierce, destructive form of Śiva, was jealous of Śaṅkara and vengefully wished to kill the philosopher. Krakaca meditated until the skull he held filled with liquor. He drank the intoxicant and then continued to meditate until the terrifying form of Śiva appeared before him. The Kāpālika asked the god to destroy Śaṅkara. "Am I to kill myself?" Śiva responded. And at once he cut off the head of Krakaca.[37]

The woman must be capable of both anger and forgiveness. The balance between repulsing the lover and yielding to him, the delicate tension, is maintained with the help of a female friend, the lady's confidante. The *brahmacārin* has a spiritual preceptor, a guru, "an ocean of mercy, a knower of *brahman*,"[38] to guide him toward liberation and instruct him in the knowledge of *brahman*. In the theory and practice of love, the loving girl has a friend to counsel her in the affairs of her heart, to act as go-between and instruct her in the ways of courtship. She is referee and coach in the erotic game, active during the separation of lovers, strategizing their reunion. If the separation is caused by parents or a spouse, the friend might carry messages of assignation; if the cause of separation is jealousy or anger she might extol each lover to the other, inspiring each to abandon pride and seek reconciliation. The friend shows the lady when to be supple and when to be impetuous:

> There are women who pretend to be innocent
> but they are stealing your husband from you
> and you do nothing at all about it;
> why are you moping about and weeping again?
> Come on, timid girl, don't give in to them.
> Wouldn't a man like yours, young and dear,
> sensitive and fond of making love, be won over
> if you'd assault him with a hundred charms—
> so harsh and wild?[39]

The poet contrasts the mature voice of the advisor, well versed in the manners of love, with that of the artless girl, new at the game:

> *The friend's instruction:*
> Why are you behaving so artlessly? You're so naive!
> Come on!
> Get tough! Be angry! Don't be so straightforward!
> Assume airs!
> > *The young girl's reply*
> > (her face reveals fear):
> > *Shhh* . . . not so loud . . .
> > my lord shall surely hear
> > since he dwells right here,
> > here within my heart.[40]

Friends urge artless girls to show anger—to play by the rules of the game. But in their innocence such girls, despite their jealousy, find it difficult to resist their lovers. Amaru describes a girl whose husband, returning home, whispers the name of one of his other mistresses. The girl pretends not to have heard but fears that her intolerant friends might find out. She looks around and seeing the room is empty she heaves a sigh of relief.[41] The innocent bride responds to her husband's transgressions with tears:

> It was the first time he had been unfaithful:
> She had not yet learned from friends the ways
> of speaking evasively, of coquettish gestures:
> > blue lotuses
> > her eyes
> > turned weeping
> > crystalline tears
> > rolling flowing
> > dripping down
> > clear cheeks.[42]

I was stubborn
    and refused to speak;
She wondered why
    and displayed her pique;
Eyes were roaming—
    a charming streak—
I laughed as if to turn
    the other cheek;
Then she shed tears
    which made me weak.[43]

"Why are you so drawn, my girl,
And why are your cheeks so pale?
And tell me why you tremble so."
    She turned away
    ". . . no reason . . ."
    and sighed and
    then the tears
    in her eyelashes
              fell. . . .[44]

    "My girl."
    "My lord?"
    "Don't be angry."
    "Have I
        shown anger?"
    "You're upset
        with me."
    "Don't worry
        it's my fault."
    "Then why
        do you weep?
        Your words
        falter."

> "Who knows
> I weep?"
> "I do."
> "What am I
> to you?"
> "My beloved."
> "I'm not
> and so
> I weep."[45]

A woman's sadness can move a man to sympathy, an aspect of love, or to a pity which is anathema to love. A friend warns her lady that "men who have fallen out of love are no longer obedient."[46] A woman's anger can push a man away so that he longs for her all the more; or it can distance him so much that he loses interest in her entirely. "Fed up with making supplication," a friend explains, men "become indifferent."[47]

There must be obstacles in the way of desire for love to be passionate, and yet the obstacles must be surmountable. Just as the guru demands that the initiate give up pride as an obstacle to the knowledge of *brahman*, so the female friend urges the young girl to abandon pride as a barrier to union with the beloved. As God speaks to the initiate through the spiritual master, the lovel seems to speak to the beloved through the friend. Guru and friend attempt to save their charges from the separation which is death. Amaru establishes a correspondence between the apocalyptic fire which is to devour the three worlds at the end of this degenerate age and the fire of love within the human heart. A friend admonishes a girl for her jealous anger:

> not thinking of the consequences
> 　　　　　　　　　　　for love
> 　not listening to your friends
> 　　　　　　　　　why girl
> are you showing anger now?
> 　　　　　　　　burning coals

flames radiant as the fires
     of apocalypse
are gathered by your own hands
      enough now
of cries in the wilderness.[48]

How fickle is your heart—
why did you ignore him?
He came home, bowed down
freely, love overflowing . . .
   And now—
As long as you live you must endure
consequences of a wretched anger—
no hope of happiness; your only refuge:
   Weeping.[49]

Your lover:
  he's scratching the ground,
   he's crouching outside—
 Oh! what a sight!
Your friends:
  their eyes are all swollen,
   they've cried, oh they've cried—
 They can't eat a bite!
Your parrots:
  they're silent, no chatter,
   all the laughter has died—
 They no longer recite!
Your self:
  you're cruel with anger,
   you're still full of pride—
 Bid it good night![50]

The friend tries to convince the woman of her lover's sincerity, his kindness and goodness. Then she goes to the man on the lady's behalf and, appealing to his sense of mercy, attempts to lure him back to his beloved with descriptions of her misery:

At once, aloud, piteously, a friend must cry:
Merciless lover
   you alone
      gave your love to her
   you alone
      cherished her so long
And now it seems to have been fate that
   you alone
      would cause this new despair
Unbearable the anger and the anguish
No words of consolation can appease it.[51]

When the friend goes to the roguish lover she herself is liable to become the object of his roguery. A lady sends her friend as a messenger to her lover, but when the go-between returns she appears to have accomplished more than her mission and the suspicious lady questions her:

"Why is your face all covered with sweat?"
"The heat of the sun posed quite a threat"
"But your eyes are wet; why are they red?"
"The words of your lover filled me with dread."
"But your hair is disheveled, why such a mess?"
"The wind was blowing I have to confess."
"And your makeup, all gone, rubbed all away?"
"Yes, rubbed off by the shawl I was wearing today."
"But your breathing is heavy; why are you tired?"
"From working so hard, doing what you desired."
"Very clever, my friend, you've not made a slip,
So tell me what rhymes with the bite on your lip."[52]

Though women must be faithful to their lovers, they may be faithless to their friends; though men must be faithful to their friends, they may be faithless to their lovers. The terms of faith, the cultural values, protect the men and keep the women vulnerable. And it is this vulnerability that provides an assurance of reconciliation.

All the confrontations, the acts of faithlessness, and the flurries of anger are for the sake of rapprochement:

> lying upon the bed
> each looked away
>   from the other
> silent suffering
>   each in their heart
> wanted to make up
>   and yet they stayed
> sullen protecting honor
>   and then
> glances mingled
>   as each looked
> at the other
>   from the corners
> of their eyes
>   with sudden laughter
> the lovers' quarrel
>   crumbled
> turning
>   embracing
> each lover
>   clung
> to the other's neck.[53]

> Love anger:
> not dispelled
> by conciliations
> not quelled
> by the words of friends
> held
> in the heart
> somehow
> hard, unfair
> all day . . .

> then though they
> looked away
> their eyes met
> smiling, laughing
> they let it go:
> Love anger.[54]

The sudden laughter, the warm smile, the deep bliss of sexual union and the intimate sharing of pleasure—this is the goal of all love, all the first glances, all the journeys and fits of pique. The lovers return to each other, merge in embraces, interpenetrate in joy.

In the religious tradition the goal of isolating oneself from one's family, the whole purpose of separation from society, is a merging in the absolute. "As milk poured into milk, oil into oil, water into water become one, united, so too the sage who knows the Self becomes Self."[55] The self returns to the Self, merges in it, and there is only being, awareness, and infinite joy. Separation exists for the sake of union.

There is a union that is as if two candles of tallow
are joined at the end so that all the light they
make is one, or that the wick, the light and the
tallow are all one; but afterwards one candle may
be separated from the other, and then there are
two candles. . . . There is another union that is
like rain falling from the sky into a river or spring,
in which case all is water and one can neither
divide nor separate the water of the river and the
water which has fallen from the sky; or it is like a
little stream entering the sea. . . .

SANTA TERESA DE JESÚS

CHAPTER FIVE

Unions

SEXUAL UNION was classified by the aestheticians into three
types according to occasion: first union, reunion after a journey,
and conciliatory union after a quarrel. The last type was generally considered the most pleasing—the unfaithful man and the
angry woman resolve separation in ardent embraces with a release of the tension which all the pretenses of courtship have
extended. Chaste or unfulfilled love was never idealized—love
was the idealization and ritualization of the feelings and actions
clustered around sexual intercourse. The sannyasi's renunciation
of his sexuality was but an aspect of his utter rejection of passion, his de-idealization and de-ritualization of feeling and desire. Amaru and Śaṅkara represent the polar attitudes within
the culture toward sexual love: it is at once the force that binds
us to the ever-decaying, ever-dying, ever-burning round of existence, and it is the force which makes that bondage enjoyable. It
is the terrible delight and the delightful terror, the fire that
comforts and the fire that consumes. The sannyasi refuses love
despite its pleasure; the poet celebrates love despite its sorrow.

For the poet, the lover, the *rasika,* love is the force of union, the energy of symphysis. Men and women joined in love discover god and goddess, Śiva-Śakti, the primordial unity which is the source of the world. But for the philosopher or the renunciate love is the expression of separation, the energy of disseverance. It results from the delusion of individuality, the notion of duality and distinction between the self and *brahman.*

Union is the goal of both the lover and the holy man, but they have opposite conceptions of union. For the former union is a momentary refuge from the tedious reality of separation: two candles come together and the flames seem as one. For the holy man union is a realization of the nonseparation of all things, the continuity and unity of the one reality: the rains return to the source and the stream flows irretrievably into the sea. For the lover the body is the means to union; for the holy man it is the obstacle. Śaṅkara utterly condemns the body as a "rotten corpse," a fetid "lump of flesh,"[1] in order to cease identifying with that which is not eternal.

Love issues opposites in equal measure: the greater the pleasure, the greater the attachment to the pleasure; the greater the attachment, the greater the pain at the inevitable passing of pleasure; the greater the pain, the greater the thirst for pleasure. . . . Love is a centrifugal force, renunciation a centripetal one. The renunciate seeks stillness and satisfaction within himself, at the very center of the spinning round of existence. The lover seeks satisfaction outside of himself despite his awareness that there can be none. His desire expands desire:

> Love had made me dry
>   so I thought I'd try
> To quench my thirst, my need,
>   by drinking up the mead
> From my lady's lip;
>   I must have made a slip:
> My thirst increased by twice
>   from kisses full of spice.[2]

The taste of the beloved's kisses is spicy, literally "salty" and, by way of a pun, "lovely"; and so the lover must experience a universal predicament—the very thing that can satisfy desire simultaneously increases it. Śaṅkara's teaching may be understood as a way out of the predicament: the renunciate, he who has no desires, attains complete satisfaction. Sexuality, for Śaṅkara, perpetuates dissatisfaction.

The polemical dispute between Śaṅkara and Maṇḍana Miśra, the legendary debate which prompted Śaṅkara to enter the body of Amaru, centers on the issue of sexuality. Maṇḍana Miśra argues for sublimation, the utilization of erotic energy for productive ends. Sexuality is valuable for producing sons, for preserving family and society. For Śaṅkara, however, these ends have little value and he accuses his adversary: "You have assumed the garb of a ritualist as a means to indulge your desire to live with women. . . . You have become a servant of woman after abandoning the service of a teacher because you are unable to maintain celibacy."[3] The performance of community and domestic sacrifices and rites is seen not as a fulfillment of Vedic injunction but as a betrayal of the true precepts of the Veda—a hypocritical attempt to justify sensuality and cleanse oneself of sins which one continues to commit. Domestic devotion is seen not as a fulfillment of one's duty and role at a particular stage in one's life but as a betrayal of one's duty to be devoted to the incarnation of truth, one's guru. Śaṅkara accuses Maṇḍana Miśra of making these betrayals out of weakness, a weakness which is both the cause and the effect of sexuality. Asceticism stores power; sexuality squanders it. The sexual sapping of power is both biological, the surrender of semen to the woman, and psychological, the surrender of will to the woman. One of Amaru's women tells a friend of the control she once had over a lover:

> If I say, "This is black, my dear,"
> he'd say, "Black it is!"
> And if I say, "No, it's actually white,"
> he'd agree, "Okay!"
> If I say, "Let's go,"
> he'd say, "Off we go!"
> And if I say, "Stop talking about going,"
> he'd agree, "Right, let's not go!"[4]

Maṇḍana Miśra, as a ritualist and a householder, defends a religious tradition which validates social persistence and esteems life in the world against Śaṅkara for whom religion is a mode of release from the world. "Having been born of woman and raised by her," Maṇḍana Miśra asked Śaṅkara, "how can you be so ungrateful as to hate women?" The renunciate replied: "Having been born of woman and suckled at her breast, how can you seek enjoyment of her like an animal?"[5] To find gratification from anything female, woman or nature, is to commit a transgression punishable by the tedious death of perpetual rebirth.

That which is dreadful to the philosopher may amuse the poet. The very forms which Śaṅkara saw as "rotten corpses" can appear to Amaru as sweet and full of life:

> In summer afternoons that are hot and calm
> Women anoint their flesh with sandal balm;
> Lips are red with betel and soft with sighs
> As they wash mascara from their dark eyes;
> Clinging robes, hair sweet with floral sprays—
> How very beautiful women are on such summer days.[6]

Sexual union is participation in that beauty, surrender to that illusion, and Amaru's lovers pursue it thirstily. For Śaṅkara such pursuits are base and bestial—only renunciation can raise us "above the level of beasts."[7] The life force perpetuates ignorance and death. But for Amaru, as a love poet, sexuality is refuge from dying, love is aesthetic wisdom, and courtship raises us above the level of beasts by transforming instinct into artful ritual.

The eroticians enumerated the rules, conventions, and manners constituting the code of this erotic ritual. Through etiquette sexual union became an art, a refinement, a cultural event. The playful and sophisticated ritual is described in the erotic treatises: the man receives the woman in a room fragrant with incense and flowers, and in the presence of friends and servants refreshments are served and music is played. The man might touch the hem of the lady's garment or the knot of her robe in order to suggest his desire. There would be discussions of art, telling of charming stories full of suggestive asides, and the recitation of love poems. The gentleman might offer his lady flowers or betel. At the appropriate moment, in due time, he would dismiss the servants and hope that friends would leave. He would embrace his lady lightly, play amorous games, and then untie the knot of her garment, careful all the while to allay any fears or fits of modesty she might have or pretend to have.[8] The image of the knot appears throughout the poems of Amaru. It is emblematic of a self-imposed separation of lovers. It begs to be untied:

> The lady's stomach was in knots that night
> And her skirt was knotted just as tight.
> Angry, she feigned sleep, she turned her face;
> Softly he touched the knot—a deft embrace.
> So cleverly had these two lovers plotted
> That both stomach and skirt became unknotted.[9]

The lover who unties the knot attains his goal: the nakedness of his beloved, the reality behind her adornments, and union. The image of the knot also appears throughout the writings of Śaṅkara—the initiate who unties the "knot of the heart" attains his goal, the reality behind all the phenomenal veils, and there is a realization of union with that reality. The knot, that which seemed to be some *thing*, substantial and real, something with shape and tangibility, is realized to be nothing but a twist and turn in something else. When the knots which are desires are untied, the naked truth is known.[10]

The *brahmacārin* traditionally left home and went into the forest to learn to untie the knots of affection and duty which kept him bound to society. Similarly the young girl of erotic poetry might leave home and go into the forest for a secret tryst with her lover, a communion which took place beyond the boundaries of society. She would move cautiously and fearfully, the darkness protecting her from the eyes of her husband or father, to the place where her lover waited. She would feel the hand of her lover touch the knot of her skirt. While in many of Amaru's poems it is ambiguous whether or not the lovers are married, it is clear in the depictions of the woman who goes to her lover at night that the union is illicit and all the more exciting for being so. Though she is an adulteress, she is not unfaithful—her fidelity is not to her husband or father (as demanded by social constraints) but to her lover (as demanded by aesthetic convention). Though the ideal man of poetry might love many women, the ideal woman loved but one man. The poetry reflects the values of a polygamous society in which economics and politics, not love and sexuality, determined marriage. A strict ethical code determined behavior in marriage; a strict aesthetic system of values determined behavior in love. They were not so much in conflict as they were mutually exclusive realms of experience. Marriage was reasonable; love was entertaining.

It became a poetic convention for the lady to go to the man. The development of this motif may reflect the cosmological vision of the female as the active force and agent in the universe. *Śakti* is the active emanation from the passive reality which is *brahman*. The still and quiet male spirit abides, hidden and imprisoned, in chaotic, restless matter. Pārvatī dances alluringly around the entranced yogi, Śiva. The *yoni*, the vulva emblematic of the goddess, turns around the *liṅga*, the phallus which symbolizes the god. The feminine wheel turns around the masculine axle.

Amaru's women seem inexperienced as they make their way
to adulterous assignations. One young girl "with thighs like ele-
phants' trunks" is encountered in the forest:

> *Where are you going on this dark cloudy night?*
>> to where he dwells,
>> the man who is dear,
>> dearer than life . . .
> *Aren't you afraid, all alone, no one in sight?*
>> isn't love, the god
>> who is armed with
>> flower-tipped arrows,
>> my bodyguard tonight?[11]

The inexperienced and even inept girl willing to risk her reputation in order to rendezvous with her lover combines the moral
virtue of innocence with the aesthetic ideal of passionate amor-
ousness—she is the innocent adulteress, the artless coquette.
One such girl who has not learned to silence her ornaments gives
herself away:

> on your bosom : silver necklace
> on your hefty hips : singing cincture
> on your feet : jingling-jewelled anklets
> on your way to your lover : tattoo & tintinnabulation
> so why, girl, do you look about with such trepidation?[12]

The woman, taking the active role in going to the man, may
remain the active agent by assuming the reverse posture and
energetically riding astride her lover. The *Kāmasūtra* recom-
mends this posture when the man is exhausted from previous
intercourse, when the woman's passion has not subsided, and
when a pleasant diversion from the ordinary mode of union is
desired. Vātsyāyana explains that with flowers falling from her
hair, with laughter interrupting her panting, the woman should
pin her beloved down, press him with her breasts, poke and dig

him with her fingers.[13] In this posture, this reversal of roles, the woman conquers and subdues the man and his joy is in submission, passivity, and reversal. She is the active goddess and he is still, unmoved like the meditating renunciate, like Śiva, the ithyphallic yogi. But while the renunciate shuns sexual intercourse for the sake of experiencing divine bliss, the lover shuns the divine for the sake of experiencing sexual delight:

> The face of a girl making love on-top:
>   forehead wet, weary eyed, she nods
> As earrings quiver and curls flip-flop.
>   Who on earth has need of the gods?
> May her face watch over you non-stop.[14]

In another poem depicting lovemaking in the reverse posture a girl suddenly becomes self-conscious and embarrassed:

> In the midst of making love
> the girl returned to her senses,
> realized what she was doing
> and got back her normal defenses:
> "Modesty's a woman's wealth,
> her only source of compensation,
> yet my anklets ringing out
> pass on the scandalous information
> that I'm a wanton girl!"
> Thus in the midst of making love
> she let go of both her dear man
> and her manly posture, up above.[15]

The phrase "she let go of her dear man," through the poet's choice of vocabulary and construction, might also be translated "her lover was liberated." The profane parodies the sacred. The lover and the renunciate mimic and embody each other.

Sexual intercourse, sensual indulgence, and meditation, sensual restraint, both lead to a unitive dissolution of the ego, a loss of distinction between inner and outer, subject and object. Śaṅkara's chaste euphoria and Amaru's carnal beatitude converge—oblivion is their mutual bliss. The lover and the renunciate, in orgasm and in spiritual realization respectively, experience a cessation of thought, an absorption and integration characterized by paramount joy, an untying of the knots, an experience transcending experience, a knowledge transcending knowing. A girl describes her union with her beloved to a friend:

> When my beloved came to bed
> My robe slipped loose of its own accord
> The skirt barely clung to my thighs
> That is all I remember now
> Once we touched I could not know who he was
> Who I was and how much less our love[16]

And a man recollects his union with his lady:

> tight–embraces–crushed–breasts–bristling–delight–
> intense–love–swelling–feeling–girdle–skirt–slipping–
> faint–whispers:
>
> no
>
> no
> too much
> no
> don't
> no
> enough
> no . . .
> "Is she asleep? is she dead? or has she disappeared—
> melted, absorbed
> into my heart . . . ?"[17]

Śaṇkara's absorption in *brahman, samādhi,* is typified by the
same ecstatic obliteration of mental activity:

> mind : disappeared
> activities : vanished
> *ātman-brahman* : oneness-realized
> I don't know : this & not-this
> I don't know : how great the joy[18]
>
> where has the world gone?
> who took it away?
> with what has it merged?
> now you see it & now you don't!
> amazing![19]

In the Vedānta system, spiritual realization or *samādhi* is classified into two species: that unitive absorption in which distinction remains *(savikalpa-samādhi)* and that in which no distinc-
tions remain *(nirvikalpa-samādhi).* The former is as when "two
candles of tallow are joined at the end so that all the light they
make is one . . . but afterwards one candle may be separated
from the other"—the practitioner realizes the nature of *brahman* as his mind acquires the formless form of *brahman;* the ego
is transformed but he remains a subject aware of an object. His
awareness of *brahman* demands a distinction and is, therefore, a separation. In *savikalpa-samādhi* the world passes and
the awareness is full of bliss, but the bliss itself can become an
obstacle—when the practitioner experiences "enjoyment of the
rasa" of the eternal he may be tempted to savor it.[20] The erotic
experience resembles this phase of *samādhi* in which the *rasa* is
enjoyed as an end in itself. The fires of love melt the ego, but
the waters of peace dissolve it. The true renunciate, in contrast
with the lover, renounces even the pleasure of his renunciation.
No ego remains. With that renunciation, with abandonment
even of the appreciation of the goal, comes *nirvikalpa-samādhi.*

"It is like rain falling from the sky into a river or spring . . . all is water and one can neither divide nor separate the water of the river and the water which has fallen from the sky." Śaṇkara explains that his "mind dissolved like a hailstone and merged with the ocean [of *brahman*]."²¹ There is only *brahman*, then, no subject realizing that it is *brahman*. And when the relative is dissolved in the absolute, the phenomenal in the transcendental, the sannyasi becomes a *jīvan-mukta*, one who is liberated while yet alive. He experiences not his own joy, not the joy of union, but the joy which is *brahman*. He is beatified:

. . . I AM ACTUALIZED I AM FULFILLED I AM LIBERATED I AM ETERNAL JOY I AM UNATTACHED I AM DISEMBODIED I AM UNMARKED I AM UNDIFFERENTIATED I AM PEACEFUL I AM PURE I AM INFINITE I AM ETERNAL I AM NOT THE ENJOYER I AM NOT THE DOER I AM IMMUTABLE I AM STILL I AM ALONE I AM . . .²²

The *jīvan-mukta* is dead in life, dead to separation and relativity, distance and sorrow, and when he dies he does not return to this world, the world of death. He is eternal because he has ceased dying, engaging in what the lover might imagine to be living. The *jīvan-mukta* knows neither pleasure nor pain, wisdom nor folly, not even bondage and liberation: "There is neither birth nor death, neither one who is bound nor one who is an adept, neither one who is liberated nor one who is striving for liberation."²³ And that ecstasy lasts forever. The lover, on the other hand, inevitably feels the revenge of time and space. He returns from his ecstasy. After lovemaking the two, who felt momentarily as one, realize their twoness once more. In *samādhi* there is no "after"—the one, which seemed through the beguiling power of *māyā* as two, realizes the truth of its oneness. "Once the knowledge of the oneness of *brahman* destroys the knowledge of twoness," Śaṅkara explains, "it cannot return."²⁴

Lover and beloved, however, always reemerge after lovemaking, always become distinct. Love demands duality, reversibility,

and repetition. Since love is a form of desire, the attainment of
its aim weakens it; thus the moments after lovemaking are a particularly dangerous time for love. Immediately after intercourse
the young lady may be embarrassed or shy:

> shaking her hand *uh-uh*
> > searching for her clothes
> she throws what's left of her flower garland
> > at the lamplight
> covers her husband's eyes
> > laughing bewildered
> after making love
> > the beautiful girl
> he stares at her again and again *uh-huh*[25]

To cope with shyness and shame and to ensure that love persists in its aftermath, Vātsyāyana advises that lovers avoid each
other's glances and behave like strangers. After washing they
should share refreshments and then reminisce about their first
meeting and the times they have had to be apart. The lady
might sit on the man's lap and let him point out the constella-
tions to her. He might rub sandal paste on her body to cool and
refresh her.[26] And such delicate behavior might arouse passion
once more:

"delicate girl, the bed is quite soiled from all the sandal
powder that came off our bodies while we were making love"
> > he urged me
> > > to lie
> > on his chest
> > > then
> > fiercely
> > > he bit my lip
> > impetuously
with those pincers, his toes, he pulled off the covers
and then all at once . . . . .once again we were lovers[27]

The sudden permutation of tenderness into violence reflects the attitudes of the *Kāmasūtra,* the "scripture" which Śaṅkara is said to have studied while embodied in the form of Amaru. Sexual intercourse is described as a "battle" both figuratively and literally, Vātsyāyana catalogs the scratches and bites which arouse and maintain passion, the methods of striking and thrashing, and the shrieks and sighs they elicit. He tells of lovers blinding, maiming, and even murdering each other in sexual combat. The man and the woman, warriors of love, are to be evenly matched according to the dimensions of their genitals, the intensity of their passion, and their ability to endure the onslaught of lovemaking, so that they can experience the same sensations at the same time—just as rams fighting, according to the text, receive the same shock on their heads if they are of equal strength. For lover and ascetic, poet and renunciate, pain and pleasure are closely related, intermingled, even confused. Vātsyāyana reconciles the ideals represented by Amaru and Śaṅkara by positing a dispassionate passion—he explains that he composed the *Kāmasūtra* only after strictly observing vows of celibacy and he warns that the indulgences described in the text must be practiced with utter restraint and detachment.[28]

The commander-in-chief of all the armed forces in the battle of love is Kāma, the god who is desire, who is born in the heart, who has dominion over this world, and who is called Death (Māra). When he attacked Śiva, the great lord of yoga opened the eye in the middle of his forehead to release the fire stored and augmented by his asceticism and it burned the god of love to ashes. But Kāma could not be defeated—bodiless he continues to torment gods, men, and beasts. Śaṅkara, as an incarnation of Śiva, is the enemy of Kāma; Amaru, as a love poet, is an ally. He honors the god who both tortures and serves all lovers:

The battle of love was over
the warriors had broken camp
   the slender girl
   sadly sighed
   distressed
   by the wait
   her lover
   had pillaged
   her clothes
On the double Generalissimo Love
Master Archer of the Universe
returned to his post at the front.[29]

The theft of the girl's clothes is at once a taking of booty after a
battle and also a prank, a trick. Sexual union is at once a battle
and a game, war and play, aggressive and regressive. Vātsyāyana
enumerates the many games which lovers should play and he
suggests that the hearts of women may be won over by playfulness.[30] Love is play. So too, for Śaṅkara, is creation, this world of
māyā.[31] And so too is poetry: the poet plays with the sentiment
and with the words, images, and conceits.

The poems depicting the aftermath of love's battle-game
make evident the literary compulsion for suggestion and indirec-
tion. The poems may present signs, evidence which lovers have
left behind, for the *rasika,* with his knowledge of poetics and
erotics, to decipher. A poem lacking any characters at all becomes, through the power of suggestion, more explicit than
direct description of intercourse:

Crushed flowers all over the creased and rumpled bedcover
Tell the positions in which she made love to her lover:
Here smeared with betel juice, juicy and red
[She must have been lying with her face on the bed];
And here there are footprints, her cosmetic lac
[He must have been lying flat on his back];
Here aloe ointments and powder sprays are the clue
[For the position see *Kāmasūtra,* chapter 6 of part 2].[32]

The poet also depicts languorous women after lovemaking; they are cooled by southern breezes laden with sandal fragrance. The wind is Kāma's ally. The world is fecund and pulsing with erotic energies:

> The wind blows each morning in the springtime
> To enrapture our hearts with perfumes, fragrant pollen
> From blue lotuses it has gently opened.
> Lovemaking's languors
> Are blown away . . . and
> The wind blows each morning in the springtime
> To caress the moon, the lovely face of each lovely girl,
> Gathering drops of sweat from their faces, shaking
> Curls and the skirts
> Across their hips . . .
> The wind blows each morning in the springtime.[33]

The skill of the poet, like the skill of the lover, was in saying what had been said countless times before in such a way that it seemed not to have been said before. Love and poetry discover what is new about the old. Ingenuity was valued as highly as sincerity. The poet plays with the image of the breezes which cool women after lovemaking; he explores the possibilities of the conceit:

> softly sweetly scented
> balmy breezes blowing
> fully flower fragranced from
> loving ladies' locks lull
> wanton women weary with
> love's lingering languor[34]

> Kissing the fawn-eyed girls, drinking their sighs,
> Caressing breasts they've rubbed with saffron dyes,
> Delighting bees, blending pollen with its snows
> To scatter them in the heavens, the wind of winter blows.[35]

One verse is a universe, a phonological cosmos with its own laws, elements, and seasons. Time and space are measured and ordered: metered. Inflection establishes connection and contrast, harmony and tension. There is a passion for structure. To order is to create. The consort of the creator of the universe, Brahmā, is Sarasvatī, goddess of speech and patroness of the literary arts; and the poet, the creator of the poem, must take her as his tutelary deity and appease, court, and seduce her.

Śaṅkara's renunciation of the world, his penetration of *māyā*, must finally include a renunciation of language. Language perpetuates illusion. The silence from which it emerges through the power of Sarasvatī, the silence to which it returns, alone is real. Silence is truth; all words are lies. "Rules of grammar cannot help you," Śaṅkara warns, "when time is finished, rolled up."[36]

> words
> turn back
> with the mind
> unable
> to attain
> IT:SILENCE
> yogis
> are able
> to attain
> IT:SILENCE
> the wise
> should
> become
> IT:SILENCE
> always . . .[37]

Bhāratī, the wife of Maṇḍana Miśra who challenged Śaṅkara with questions on the erotic arts and sciences, is said by the hagiographer to have been an incarnation of Sarasvatī. The goddess was cursed with a human birth for having laughed at the way one of the divine sages chanted the Vedic hymns—cursed to remain human until encountering Śiva in the form of the earthly sage Śaṅkara. The goddess of poetry puts the holy man to the most difficult test of all: he cannot claim wisdom unless he understands human love and sexuality, and yet he cannot ascend the throne of wisdom unless he is chaste. He must prove his wisdom and take his place on the throne in order to establish Vedānta on earth and fulfill the purpose of his descent.[38] Śaṅkara can learn of love without impurity only by using the body of Amaru—the holy man *needs* the lover, the poet. The philosopher needs words to explore the silence, language to describe what cannot be described. In the end there is silence again. Words flow into it as light flows into darkness, as heat flows into cold. It cannot be reversed.

The silence of love and the silence of renunciation are utterly different. The silence which follows lovemaking must make the lover anxious—it might indicate disappointment, anger, melancholy, or words that cannot be uttered. The silence of love is transient. The silence of *samādhi* is peaceful—it indicates understanding, awareness, realization of that truth from which all words turn back. When the silent sage, the *muni,* speaks it is out of compassion; it is with detachment that he breaks the eternal silence which he knows. The lover speaks out of passion and necessity, aching for a response.

The silence of love and the silence of renunciation are utterly different and yet they sound exactly the same.

Water and fire succeed
The town, the pastures and the weed.
Water and fire deride
The sacrifice that we denied.
Water and fire shall rot
The marred foundations we forgot,
Of sanctuary and choir.
This is the death of water and fire.
                                    T. S. ELIOT

CHAPTER SIX

Dissolutions

THERE IS AN INDIAN STORY of a queen who, walking in the woods, became lost. As dusk approached she became afraid and rushed about frantically, hoping to find her way home. A demon, perched in a tree, watched and desired her. He disguised himself as her husband and when he appeared before her in the form of the king, she embraced him gratefully and lovingly, relieved of her fears. The demon caressed her and began to untie the knot of her shawl. Out of modesty she resisted, pleading for him to wait until they returned home. He admonished her—it is a wife's duty to be obedient to her husband, to give herself to her lord whenever and wherever he wishes. She submitted and he enjoyed her on the ground in the dark forest. When he had taken his pleasure he stood over her and as she looked up at him, she saw the guise fall away. The demon laughed at her and announced that from their union would come a son, half-demon and half-human, Kaṃsa, the enemy of Kṛṣṇa.

Traditional Indian society demanded that a woman be obedient to her husband—compulsory submissiveness was sanctified in the domestic treatises, making marital devotion the fundamental form of female religious practice. In wholly surrendering to the will of her husband, a woman gained spiritual merit as well as security and protection from the harshness of the world. She also became vulnerable to her husband's potential greed, cruelty, or indifference. The woman cannot be certain that the husband or lover who embraces her will not suddenly stand over her laughing, that demonic impulses will not suddenly be revealed. In a world which is illusion there is no knowing what face is behind the mask, which gestures are false, and which feelings are real. Love imperils the woman, pulls her to the brink of death:

                              for a long time
            she watched him eyes fearful
            she begged him   hands clasped
                              in supplication
                              and then
            she clung to him the edge of his robe
            she embraced him no pretenses
                              and when
                              her lover
                              cruel and faithless
                              spurned her
                              started to leave
            she let go first of her will to live
            she let go then   of the man she loved[1]

            The Lord, Love,
        cruel when lovers are apart,
            starves me at will;
            The Lord, Death,
        cunning in counting my days
            refuses to show mercy;
            My Lord, *You*,
        diseased with arrogance—
            ask yourself how women in love,
            delicate as fresh tendrils,
                are to endure.[2]

The woman is abandoned in her most fragile and vulnerable condition: the open and supple state which she has cultivated in order to please the man. The traditionally idealized goal of a woman's life was to serve and comfort a man and to be accessible to him. The man's goal was freedom from attachment to the pleasure and comfort of woman and domestic life for the sake of access to something absolute. After the debate with Śaṅkara, Maṇḍana Miśra renounced the life of the householder to strive for liberation, and his wife was obliged to let him go. The very same sense of duty which makes woman cling to man finally impels her to release him. Abandonment is woman's destiny:

> *my breasts*
> just budding
> became full
> against your chest
> in embraces.
> *my words*
> once artless
> lost their innocence
> influenced by your wit
> your clever repartee.
> *my arms*
> let go
> of my mother's neck
> that they might
> cling to you.
> *my deceiver—*
> what can I do?
> you do not even walk
> down my street
> any more.[3]

In the beginning love is marked by anxiousness, in the end by regrets. Love and time conspire to deplete the heart. Delight withers with age. Without the innocent energy of youth, amorous playfulness yields to domestic dreariness. If a woman succeeds in avoiding abandonment, her only reward is disenchantment. One of Amaru's women recollects a time when love was fresh, when the coquettish anger of love "was expressed in a frown and chastisement in silence . . . and then a glance made everything all right and we apologized by smiling at each other." But with time and age she laments over the transience of feeling and passion: "Look at the ruination of the love that once was—you wallow at my feet and I, obstinate woman that I have become, cannot let go of my indignation."[4]

Lovers must finally hear Śaṅkara: "Infatuation over such things as the body is a vast death."[5] Desolation is the fruit of love. The demon laughs.

> bond of love—gone
> affection and respect—dissolved
> true feeling—vanished
> the man in front of me—like any man
> I think of it,
> my friends,
> I think of days gone by
> and I do not know why
> my heart
> does not break
> into a hundred pieces.[6]

> Stop, I know you now:
> no more empty words;
> leave me alone, my love,
> It's not your fault—it's fate
> that has turned against me;
> since your love, once strong,
> could come to such a sad state
> as this, how can it hurt me if
> my life, fleeting by nature and
> wretched, is over? It is too late.[7]

The personal experience of love, like the flesh it animates, must ultimately fade, die, and be forgotten. But love as a poetic sentiment, aesthetic ideal and cultural institution, can persist. Amaru the poet is the guardian of that persistence. The poems are not arranged sequentially or chronologically—they do not follow the temporal progression from the awakening of love to its dissolution. They are, rather, collected together in a timeless and seemingly random order—the poems of sorrow, isolation, and disenchantment are scattered amidst the mirthful and fanciful poems celebrating the pleasantness of love and the charm of the sensual life. As joy leads to sorrow, sorrow leads to joy. The overall effect is one of affirmation. The poet validates the world and the body, sensuality and desire. He affirms love not only despite its futility but also, perhaps, because of it.

The philosopher sees the fluctuations of feeling as symptomatic of the unrealness of emotion and, because of this unrealness, this unreliability, he rejects human feeling. The sentimental cycle of joy-sorrow-joy-sorrow . . . is itself sorrowful. Śaṅkara negates it in order to become firmly established in an unfluctuating and eternally reliable reality "which consists of joy and does not consist of sorrow."[8] All the pleasures of the world are a great misery for they tempt one to identify with the body and personality, with name and form, and in that identification one becomes careless about the one true Self. From "this carelessness comes delusion and then egoism and then bondage and then misery."[9] Within the phenomenal realm everything generates its opposite: birth yields death, pleasure yields pain, and the joy of union yields the sorrow of isolation:

> as this flesh at first
> was one and undivided
> so then it was that
> all my hopes were crushed
> and no longer
> were you my lover
> was I your beloved

and now? what next?
what shall be the fruit
of such a life
so diamond-hard?[10]

While the lover must always return from unity to division, from
love to despair, the holy man knows an absolute bliss of unity
from which, Śaṅkara promises, there is no return. The joy of
brahman transcends the world and has no opposite.

In order to experience that transcendental joy one must be
willing to renounce the world. The aspirant calls out to his preceptor: "Save me from death! I am afflicted by the unquenchable forest fire of this world!"[11] The fires of love which perpetuate existence are, for Śaṅkara, appalling fires of death. Death is
the price we pay for our flesh; despair is the price we pay for our
joy in this world: "As long as one has any regard for the body, a
living corpse, he is impure and sure to suffer from birth, death,
and disease. . . . Know that death is quick to overwhelm one
who walks the insidious paths of sensual pleasure. . . . Conquer
that vast death which is your infatuation over your body, your
wife and children. . . . Give up the notion of the self as being
that pile of excrement which is your flesh, fat, and bones; identify with the absolute, *brahman,* the Self of all, and then you
shall attain the highest *peace.*"[12]

The renunciate gives up love and shuns all passion for the
sake of that peace; the lover gives up that peace, shuns the absolute, for the sake of human warmth. The renunciate's peace is in
deliverance from death, the realization that the destruction of
the body does not affect the real Self any more than "the falling
of a leaf" affects a tree.[13] Śaṅkara did not die—the illusory body
dissolved and yet, according to the hagiographer, "he remains
even today in the form of an all-pervading consciousness."[14]

The lover's passion is equally a response to death. When
Amaru died his wives wept bitterly; when he appeared to come
back to life they rejoiced and clung to him with urgency, trying
to savor the sweetness of love while it lasted.

The lover and the renunciate converge in the legend of Amaru and Śaṅkara. The legend reconciles the antithetical ideals, love and renunciation, by suggesting a third, higher ideal—that of reconciliation itself. A legendary figure, a wise and peaceful spirit in a beautiful and delighted body, enjoys the world lovingly, passionately, and yet with detachment and understanding. He is aware of the transience of the world but can take pleasure in it nevertheless because he is conscious of something constant and sacred permeating the world.

The fires of love and the waters of peace converge in the myth of a submarine fire. Śiva had immolated the god of love with the erotic fire he had stored within through ascetic practices. Once released, the seething, shooting, wild fire, taking the form of a raging, galloping mare, threatened to incinerate the universe. Brahmā, the creator, appealed to the ocean to take the fire into its depths that heaven and earth might be spared. The ocean received it and there, according to the myth, it continues to burn. The image of the fire under water provides a symbol of reconciliation and harmonization of opposites: "Wonderful is the submarine fire! Wonderful is the glorious sea! Thinking of their greatness, the mind quakes," the poet Keśaṭa sings:

> The fire consumes the ocean,
>   the sea in which it's drenched,
> and yet it is unslakable—
>   its thirst is never quenched;
> The ocean is consumed by fire,
>   the flames that it contains,
> and yet it is so very vast—
>   that every drop remains.[15]

But at last the apocalyptic flames, the fire under water, consumes the ocean and burns itself out. Nothing remains. Beyond the world, time and space, the round of birth and death, there is nothing. The love celebrated in the poetry of Amaru transforms the world into a refuge from that nothingness; the teachings of Śaṅkara transform that nothingness into a refuge from the world.

The poet must invent love as a consolation for the sorrow that is inevitable in a heart that cannot renounce the world. The philosopher must invent truth for the sorrow that it is inevitable in one who sees the vanity of human striving in a world of change. Each bears the burden of his vision. The ascetic is always in danger of temptation and must stay on guard against the alluring delights of the world. The lover is always in danger of awakening, of seeing the abyss, and must stay on guard against the terrible thought of what must inevitably come.

Nothing outlasts the death of fire and water. Despite passion or wisdom, love or renunciation, all will be absorbed into oblivion. But until then the poems of Amaru and the teachings of Śaṅkara, in different ways, offer solace and a hope for endurance. Until then the fires in which we are to be burned away may warm us and give us light; the waters in which our ashes will be scattered and dissolved may quench our thirst and cleanse us.

Notes

ABBREVIATIONS

AG   Ānandagiri. *Śaṅkaravijaya.* Edited by J. Tarkapañcānana. Biblioteca Indica. Calcutta: Baptist Mission Press, 1968.

AŚ   *Amaruśataka* with the commentary of Arjunavarmadeva *(Rasikasaṃjīvanī).* Edited by M. P. Durgāprasāda and K. P. Parab. Kāvyamālā no. 18. Bombay: Nirṇaya-Sāgara Press, 1900.

MV   Mādhavācārya. *Śaṅkaradigvijaya* with the commentary of Dhanapatisūri *(Ḍiṇḍima).* Ānandāśrama Series no. 22. Poona: Ānandāśrama Press, 1915.

SG   *Śrīśaṅkaragranthāvali.* 11 vols. Śrīraṅgam: Vāṇi-Vilāsa Press, 1952–1960.

SVM   *Śrīśaṅkaravijayamakaranda* [texts compiled from the traditional biographies of Śaṅkara]. Edited by S. V. Radhakrishna Sastri. Trichy: Vāṇi-Vilāsa Press, 1978.

VCM   *Vivekacūḍāmaṇi.* Edited in *Śrīśaṅkaragranthāvali* (SG) 10:1–100.

CHAPTER I

1. VCM 580.
2. MV 9; AG 58–59; Ravicandra gives the legend in his commentary on AŚ.
3. AŚ 2. Śaṃbhu, "Beneficent One," the particular epithet of Śiva used by the poet in this stanza, suggests a paradox which is the very essence of the god —his benevolence often expresses itself through his terrible fury.

4. *Bhagavadgītabhāṣya,* ed. A. Mahadeva Shastri (Madras, 1961) 3.37–39.
5. *Nirvāṇaṣaṭka,* SG 11:394.
6. AŚ 1. Rama Nath Sharma has suggested to me a very different way of construing the verse: looking at the scratches she has made on Śiva's hand during lovemaking, the goddess is "amused by the nail marks shimmering on the back of his hand when it is fixed in the *khaṭakāmukha* position to stretch the bowstring."
7. *Vedasāraśivastotra,* SG 11:63.
8. *Saundaryalaharī,* ed. W. Norman Brown (Cambridge, Mass., 1958), 35.
9. Ibid., 100.
10. AŚ 102. Literally: "She is in the house and she is in all directions; she is in front and she is behind; she is on the bed and she is on every path of me as I suffer with separation from her *(or* with nonintegration with It, meaning *brahman).* Oh! Oh! O mind! There is no other reality! She is who she is! She! She! She! She is the entire world! What is this nonduality? *(or* What is this?— The Monist [Advaita] Philosophy!)"
11. MV 9.90–100. Śaṅkara explains further that he is not in danger of breaking continence in that he has mastered the yogic practice of *vajroli,* the contraction of muscles and vessels in the penis which permits the yogi to prevent loss of semen during sexual intercourse. The retained semen is to be redirected through the rest of the yogi's body for the sake of power.
12. AŚ 138. The poem can be literally translated in two ways: "This pearl necklace rolls about on the round breasts of the deer-eyed women—if this is the unsettled state of pearls *(muktā),* what about us, the slaves of love?" *or* "This pearl necklace rolls about on the round breasts of the deer-eyed women —if this is the loose behavior (or fickleness) of liberated men *(mukta),* what about us, the slaves of love?"
13. AŚ 126. The white flowers here are *kandala* blossoms which bloom suddenly and profusely at the onset of the monsoon season, a season always suggestive of the erotic mood—not only does rain bring fertility to the earth but men stay indoors with their women during the rainy season. Asceticism was believed to prevent rain; lovemaking was thought to prompt it. Compare AŚ 118:

> Raindrops:
> faintly mark the sand and peacocks,
> ever more eager, watch them fall;
> they are scattered by the winds,
> the sighs of very poor housewives;
> raindrops fall from new clouds—
> the delight of the rainy season—
> drops like soma from the moon—
> faces of women, pale from love's
> separation.

CHAPTER 2

1. AŚ 63. The exclamatory "mother!" is used here simply as an interjection, like the Italian *"mama mia!"*

2. Ibid., 110.

3. MV 4.34.

4. Ibid., 5.83.

5. Ibid., 2.68–69.

6. AŚ 4.

7. Ibid., 104. The poet plays upon various meanings of *rasa*—it can refer to sap flowing in the lotus stalk, to the water flowing in the river, to nectar or the taste of nectar, to love or that sentiment as a formalized aesthetic mood. Just as the longing of love can be candidly expressed in the presence of parents, skilled lovers can carry on a quarrel discreetly: "In the presence of the elders . . . she indicated the direction of her rival with a motion of her creeperlike brow . . . and when her face glowed, her cheeks red with anger, he fell at her feet by means of his glance" (AŚ 83).

8. Ibid., 100.

9. Ibid., 34.

10. The shower of gold fruit (MV 4.21-38; AG 3) and the diversion of the river (MV 5.1-9; AG 3), both representing a reversal of the normally dependent relationship between boy and maternal figure, emphasize Śaṅkara's innate freedom from the female power. Both incidents are connected with local legends in Kerala; some distance from Kālati, the supposed birthplace of Śaṅkara, there is a canal which is said to be the diverted river; there is a house in the same village, known as the "house of gold," which is believed to have been the home of the woman who offered the fruit to the young sannyasi.

11. *Gaṅgāstotra,* ed. Swami Sivananda (in *Mother Ganges* [Rishikesh, 1962]), pp. 17–18.

12. AŚ 135.

13. *Aparokṣānubhuti* (SG 10:383–402) 70, 95–96.

14. VCM 277-285.

15. AŚ 64.

16. Ibid., 137. "Holy water" *(lāvaṇya-vāri)* might more literally be rendered as "waters of beauty" or "salty water"; the salty water suggests the perspiration on the beloved's breasts which would sprinkle the lover during lovemaking in the conventionally preferred inverse posture. I give "well-formed thighs" for the more graphic "thighs like banana tree trunks."

17. *Aparokṣānubhuti* 48.

18. VCM 110.

19. AŚ 41. The line "he reached . . . she pulled back" might, through a grammatical ambiguity which perhaps expresses a psychological ambiguity, be translated: "[although] *she* wanted a passionate embrace, she pulled her limbs away gently."

20. Ibid., 27.

21. Ibid., 108.

22. *Aparokṣānubhuti* 4.

23. AŚ 82. The poet includes another stanza which presents practically the same scene reported in the first person: "Immediately after my friends left, saying, 'You ought to sleep, for he is asleep,' I, possessed by love, trembling, placed my mouth upon his mouth; when I saw the rogue's goose bumps, I realized he had just closed his eyes to pretend to be asleep; I was embarrassed, but he cured me of that embarrassment with steps which were appropriate to the occasion" (AŚ 37).

24. MV 9.94–96.

25. AŚ 98. I have followed the variant reading of Vemabhūpala; Arjunavarmadeva's spicier reading changes the poem's tone substantially—suddenly the girl confesses: "And I, my friend, bit him hard upon his lower lip."

26. Ibid., 16. The girl literally takes off her ruby earring and places it in the parrot's mouth under the pretext that it is a pomegranate seed. I give "ended Polly's life" for the more literal "stopped the speech of the house parrot." Compare AŚ 117: "When the parrot whispered, 'fetch food for me or else I'll tell all of your secret conduct out loud,' the face of the bride, laughing to herself, was bent down in great embarrassment like a half-open lotus bent over by a bee. Her face is captivating!"

27. Ibid., 127.

28. MV 5.10–19; SVM, p. 57.

29. *Dvādaśapañjarikāstotra*, SG 11:282–287.

CHAPTER 3

1. MV 14.80. Śaṅkara compares the life of the householder and that of the sannyasi—the renunciate's disciples are said to be his children, his body is his home, his wife is the eternal Self.

2. Ibid., 5.54–58; AG 3; SVM 5.53–59.

3. AŚ 12. "Morning" for "end of the [first] watch." The Indian day is divided into four three-hour watches from 3 A.M. to 6 P.M.

4. Ibid., 103.

5. *Aparokṣānubhuti* 106–109.

6. AŚ 62.

7. MV 5.57–58.

8. AŚ 132. Literally:

He: "My dear lady, you'll have to spend several days with your eyes closed."

She: "Good-bye, good-bye! I'll close my eyes until the roads are empty in all directions!"

He: "I'll return."
She: "You will return to increase the fortunes of your friends."
He: "Tell me what you want."
She: "A funeral offering at the sacred bathing places!"

The woman's initial attempt to pretend that she is not troubled by the man's departure, that she wants him to do what he must do, finally gives way to her confession that without him she will die. In these scenes of parting, lovers continually contradict themselves. "Go" means "stay," "I'm happy" means "I'm sad," and "I'm a hypocrite" means "I'm being truthful":

> I heard the resolute words of my lover, all set to part—
> "I'm leaving . . ."
> I watched him go far, far away—
> stopping, he turned for a moment;
> I abide in desolation with the world once more—
> yet the breath of life is strong;
> I cherish life. . . . Wait, my friends—
> it is out of hypocrisy that I weep. [AŚ 79]

9. Ibid., 10.
10. Ibid., 61.
11. Ibid., 35. When the woman's beloved leaves she grows thin and thus her bracelets "depart"—they slip off and her tears fall. The bracelets are the lover's "dear friends" in that they are gone when he is gone and they return with him.
12. MV 10.36–61.
13. *Carpaṭapañcarikāstotra*, SG 11:281.
14. Ibid., vv. 14–16.
15. MV 5.59–74; cf. SVM 8.60–78; AG 3. The incident is traditionally explained with the story of a *gāndharva* named Hāhā who was cursed by the sage Durvāsa; he was transformed into a crocodile and made to stay in that form until he could take hold of the foot of Śiva.
16. VCM 79–80.
17. *Kaupīnapañcaka*, SG 11:420–421.
18. MV 5.126–127.
19. Ibid., 5.122. This motif, the jealousy and loss of power of the Vedic god Indra, is a feature of both the mythology of Kṛṣṇa and the legend of the Buddha. Indra blames Kṛṣṇa and the Buddha respectively for causing people to neglect sacrifices to him.
20. Ibid., 5.138; SVM 11.
21. AŚ 54. Hearing the longing in the traveler's voice, the people give up the foolish pride which keeps lovers separated unnecessarily and they no longer mention the life-robbing word "leaving." They perform a funeral salutation to

that pride and the words of parting. The coming of the rains at a time when the traveler is still far away distresses the wife as much as it does the traveler: "When she suddenly heard the thunder of a fresh raincloud at midnight, her limbs became languid and she fell out of bed; her saddened friends supported her with their hands. She cried out anxiously and teardrops were scattered on her firm breasts; remembering again and again her beloved, the traveler's wife wept with faltering and tender words" (AŚ 129).

22. Ibid., 13. Literally: "Hearing the deep sound of a raincloud, pouring forth its water at night, a traveler brooded for a long time over the beloved lady who was separated from him; weeping with a deeply drawn sigh, he cried out at the top of his voice all night long in such a way that the villagers forbid travelers from ever staying in the village again."

23. While the Śaṅkara of the legends is dedicated to spreading the truth of *brahman* throughout India for the sake of all people, Śaṅkara the philosopher insists that the knowledge which is a means to liberation should only be given to "pure brahmins" (VCM 2 ff.).

24. The dialogue between Śaṅkara and the untouchable has been edited by T.M.P. Mahadevan (Madras, 1967) as the *Manīṣāpañcaka;* the text of the hymn is given in SG 11:416–417.

25. MV 14.22 ff.

26. AŚ 99.

27. Ibid., 76.

28. Ibid., 78.

29. Ibid., 86.

30. Ibid., 134.

31. Ibid., 77.

32. Ibid., 44. The couple literally "mounted the night," an expression which, as Kenneth Langer has pointed out to me, suggests that they "feel on top of the world" like, according to the commentator Arjuna, "an arrogant person mounting an elephant."

33. Ibid., 45.

34. Ibid., 88.

35. *Saundaryalaharī* 45.

36. MV 14.29–50.

37. *Śivanāmāvalyaṣṭaka* (SG 11:101–102) 1, 3, 5, 7.

38. *Viṣṇuṣaṭpadī* (SG 11:279) 2, 6.

CHAPTER 4

1. MV 2.36; AG 2.

2. MV 7.1–59; AG 52. The account of the legend given in a popular "comic-book" biography of Śaṅkara (*Amar Chitra Katha* no. 60) stresses the social mission of Śaṅkara: "Then [in Śaṅkara's lifetime], as now, the disrup-

tive forces of religion, race, caste, and language threatened to weaken the fabric of the one nation that is India." Śaṅkara's philosophical monism takes on political implications and ramifications; at one point the young philosopher clenches his fist and thinks to himself: "Spiritual unity comes first. National unity will follow. As a sannyasi I shall achieve this."

3. *Kāmasūtra* of Vātsyāyana, ed. M. P. Durgāprasāda (Bombay, 1900), 5.1.16; 2.10.46.

4. AŚ 49.

5. Ibid., 19.

6. Ibid., 109.

7. Ibid., 60. Compare: "You embrace me and I am unhappy; I turn away, unknowing, from the insult. What has been gained, my deceitful one, by the transgressions which have brought our happy married life to such a state? Look at your chest! It is red with dye from being pressed against the breasts of your mistress and it is branded with imprints of a braid, filthy stains of sesame oil unguent!" (AŚ 17).

8. Ibid., 26. I have translated quite freely here. The stanza might be more literally rendered: " 'Why,' she asked, 'is your chest, marked with impressions made by embraces against the surface of her thickly ointmented breasts, hidden under the pretext of bowing down at my feet?' Asking 'where is it?' I suddenly embraced her with passion to rub off the stain and, enraptured, the slender lady forgot all about it." The tension between his faithlessness (expressed by the stains on his chest) and his devotion (expressed by his obeisance) is resolved by passion—the sudden embrace which hides his profligacy in forgetfulness. Compare: "The lover, whose lower lip had been carelessly bitten by another woman, was struck by the lotus with which his beloved was playing; he stood blinking his eyes as if they had been infested with a lotus filament; his dear lady, her moonlike face puckered like a bud, stood blowing air [to remove the filament from his eye] with confusion [falling for his trick], at which point he kissed her roguishly without any bowing down in supplication" (AŚ 72).

9. Ibid., 46.

10. MV 6.64–71; SVM 13.1–13.

11. MV 8.14–31. The philosophers attempt literally to outwit each other with intentional misunderstandings based on various puns. When Maṇḍana asks Śaṅkara if he is inebriated, if "toddy has been drunk *(pīta),*" the philosopher responds, "No, toddy is not yellow *(pīta),* it is white."

12. AŚ 133. Compare: "The ornamental design on your cheek has been worn away by the clutch of your palm: the nectar of your lip, the essence of immortality, has been evaporated by your sighs; the tears, lodged in your throat, constantly make the surface of your breasts tremble—unfriendly lady— anger has become your beloved, not I!" (AŚ 81).

13. Ibid., 22.

14. The *Saundaryalaharī* attributed to Śaṅkara (but, like the devotional

hymns, clearly postdating the Śaṅkara who wrote the commentaries on the *Upaniṣads* and the philosophical treatises) extols all parts of the goddess's body with tropes and figures from the literary tradition. She is a paragon of beauty.

15. AŚ 51-52. Literally: "In the presence of the slender girl I was frightened because I had uttered the name of another woman by mistake. When I looked down out of embarrassment and began to draw something, I was cursed by fate—my drawing was somehow changed in such a way that *she* appeared there! It was indeed her again, the young woman with all her features [drawn by mistake]! After that the clever girl began to realize what was going on. Blushing, her cheeks burning red, she suddenly stammered hoarsely from mounting affection. In tears she said, 'Oh! A picture! A picture has appeared!' In anger she placed her left/cruel/beautiful foot upon my head—it was Brahmā's missile of destruction!"

16. VCM 227-228.

17. Ibid., 218.

18. AŚ 120.

19. Ibid., 55.

20. Ibid., 28. Compare: "Hearing his name, my body bristles all over with delight; seeing his moonlike face, my body acts like the moonstone [which melts under moonbeams]. Once the lord of my life approaches and stands near to embrace me, my jealous thoughts, so diamond hard, are shattered once more" (AŚ 59).

21. Ibid., 11. Compare: "I've prepared a show of anger: I've practiced bending my brow in a scowl for a long time; I've learned to shut my eyes; I've zealously studied how to stop smiling; I've mastered keeping silent; somehow I've made my mind firm and I'm composed. My success, though, will depend on fate" (AŚ 97).

22. Ibid., 73.

23. Ibid., 39.

24. Ibid., 25.

25. Ibid., 47. The entire stanza reads:

> She expects me to throw myself at her feet—
>   she covers them respectably with her dress;
> So too she hides the coming smile with a pretense—
>   she won't look me in the eyes;
> And when I speak she turns to a friend—
>   to talk in words of contradiction.
> Long live the ardent love of the slender girl—
>   even her fury is displayed with charm.

26. Ibid., 21.

27. Ibid., 36. I have followed the variant of Vemabhūpala; in Arjuna's read-

ing the woman's anger is provoked when the man bites her lip. The reference in the poem is to the gods who, in their battle against the demons, turned to Viṣṇu to obtain the gift of immortality; he directed them to churn the nectar of immortality from the cosmic ocean.

28. *Ātmabodhaprakarana* (SG 11:402–411) 68.

29. AŚ 116. Compare: "The offended lady, her eye quivering impetuously, put her foot upon his head: it was like a sign of beauty; it shone in the night; dyed with lac, it was radiant with a loveliness that surpassed the hundred-petaled lotus; it was ornamented with an anklet and crimson with its own great splendor" (AŚ 128).

30. Ibid., 9.

31. Ibid., 18. Compare: "Smiling sweetly, you greet me from afar. You take my commands deferentially and though you answer me, your gaze becomes empty; and so it is that my heart burns. Cruel woman! You conceal your anger within—this is hypocrisy!" (AŚ 14).

32. Ibid., 114. Compare: "Tired, she does not struggle as she did before when he loosens her clothes; she does not furrow her brow or bite her lip hard as he pulls her hair; she surrenders without resistance and her limbs yield during his passionate embrace: unusual as it is, this is how she shows her anger now" (AŚ 106).

33. Though the popular tradition holds that Śaṅkara taught loving devotion to god as a method of liberation (and such devotion is clearly the basis of many hymns later attributed to him), the seemingly more authentic texts defend devotion, *bhakti,* only if it is dispassionate and detached. Śaṅkara defines *bhakti* as "inquiry into the nature of one's self" (VCM 31).

34. AŚ 92.

35. Ibid., 15. Literally: "When I said 'go away,' I was just pretending to be angry but that cruel-hearted man left the bed rashly—he was gone indeed—and now my shameless heart longs for him again, that pitiless one whose love is no more. What shall I do?"

36. Ibid., 87. Compare: "He lost interest in trying to win her favor when she repulsed him as he fell at her feet in obeisance; and he was hardened when she said, 'You're behaving like a deceitful rogue!' But as her lover was leaving she looked to her friends with tears in her eyes, sighing and pounding her breast" (AŚ 20). And: " 'What a foolish girl I was,' the young woman thought, recollecting her behavior as a new bride. 'Why didn't I cling to the neck of the lord of my life? Why did I turn my head away when he kissed me? Why didn't I look at him? Why didn't I speak to him?' As the woman began to feel regret, affection took over and she knew the taste of love" (AŚ 58).

37. MV 15.1–29. In a similar legend (MV 9.1–28) a Kāpālika informs Śaṅkara that Śiva has promised him a place in heaven if he can obtain the head of either a king or a sage. Śaṅkara offers his own head, but as the Kāpālika raises his sword, Padmapāda chants a mantra which induces the man-lion avatar of Viṣṇu to manifest and destroy the wicked Kāpālika.

38. VCM 15.

39. AŚ 8. The phrase "stealing your husband" might also be translated "obtaining sexual delight," which of course they do by stealing the man.

40. Ibid., 70.

41. Ibid., 75. Compare: "In front of her cheating husband she quickly recited the lies her friends had taught her; but then she began to do what Love wished, and that certain natural manner of love, ornamented with her innocence, was charming" (AŚ 48).

42. Ibid., 29.

43. Ibid., 24.

44. Ibid., 50. Compare: "The beloved man spoke in this way to his bride: 'My lovely one, this is you (isn't it?): a woman trapped in delusion by the many worries she has to bear; her anger is apparent and alarming; her ornaments are nothing but her natural beauty and humility.' The girl, tormented with jealousy, answered somehow, stammering as she tried to hold back the tears, 'It's nothing, really. . . .' How very much she leaves unsaid" (AŚ 65–66).

45. Ibid., 57.

46. Ibid., 91.

47. Ibid., 5.

48. Ibid., 80. The "fires of apocalypse" refer to the dissolution of the universe at the end of the current degenerate age; Viṣṇu, according to one version of the myth, will take on the form of devouring Rudra and drink up all the moisture in the world and then the seven solar rays will become seven suns to set the three worlds on fire and consume them.

49. Ibid., 56.

50. Ibid., 7.

51. Ibid., 6.

52. Ibid., 113.

53. Ibid., 23.

54. Ibid., 42.

55. VCM 566.

CHAPTER 5

1. "Give up identification with this lump of flesh . . . that is like a rotten corpse" (VCM 296–297).

2. AŚ 130. Literally: "Ever since I, thirsty on account of love, drank the love/nectar from my beloved's lip, my thirst has doubled. What's so strange about that? The taste was very lovely/salty."

3. MV 8.25–31.

4. AŚ 94 (a,b).

5. MV 8.25–31.

6. AŚ 124. A fountain is muddied by the women's mascara.

7. *Aparokṣānubhuti* 130.

8. *Kāmasūtra* 2.8.5; 2.10.1–12.

9. AŚ 112. Literally: "The fair-bodied lady turned away in anger, closing her eyes in a sleep which was evidently a pretense, while her lover, skillful in embraces, reached her body with his body; when he softly touched the knot of her skirt, his hand trembling fearfully, she contracted her waist [so that he could unfasten the garment more easily]."

10. VCM 363, 558.

11. AŚ 71.

12. Ibid., 31.

13. *Kāmasūtra* 2.8.1–3.

14. AŚ 3. The poet literally asserts that there is no need for one to supplicate Brahmā, Viṣṇu, or Śiva, the Creator, Preserver, or Destroyer—her face, looking down at her lover, will "watch over" him and grant blessings. The closeness of her face, its immanence, is its sanctity. Similarly the *Saundaryalaharī* (1), attributed to Śaṅkara, suggests that Brahmā, Viṣṇu, and Śiva are dependent upon the female. The idealized female of the literary tradition became the divinized female of the devotional tradition: "If Śiva is united with *śakti* he has power; if not, the god cannot even move. . . . Viṣṇu, Śiva, Brahmā, and the other gods must propitiate you."

15. AŚ 89.

16. Ibid., 101.

17. Ibid., 40.

18. VCM 481. The steps to *samādhi* delineated in the *Aparokṣānubhuti* (102–131) represent a Vedāntic adaption of Patañjali's *Yogasūtra:* control of the senses; control of the mind; renunciation; silence; posture; steadiness of vision; control of the vital breaths; self-withdrawal; concentration; meditation on the Self; and finally *sāmadhi,* the absorption or integration which is defined as "the complete forgetfulness of all thought by first making it changeless and then identifying it with *brahman.*"

19. Ibid., 483.

20. *Aparokṣānubhuti* 126.

21. VCM 482, passim.

22. Ibid., 488–490.

23. Ibid., 574.

24. *Brahmasūtrabhāṣya,* ed. R. Halasyanatha Sastri (Bombay, 1908), 1.1.4.

25. AŚ 90.

26. *Kāmasūtra* 2.10.13 ff.

27. AŚ 74.

28. *Kāmasūtra* 7.2.57. On the violence of sexual battle see 2.4, 5, 7.

29. AŚ 115. That Love "returned to his post" suggests sexual arousal—the "post of love" being a technical term for an erogenous zone.

30. *Kāmasūtra* 1.3, 4; 2.3.15–20; 3.3.7.

31. *Brahmasūtrabhāṣya* 2.1.33.
32. AŚ 107. My bracketed comments follow the commentator's explanations of the various positions indicated in the poem, positions he describes with citations from the *Kāmasūtra:* the betel juice on the bed suggests, he notes, the *karipada* posture, an *aiba* position in which the woman bends forward and the man stands behind her; the lac on the bed indicates that her feet were on the bed, that she was astride her lover.
33. Ibid., 123.
34. Ibid., 121. Literally: "Nightly the [summer] winds, soothing to loving women who are exhausted from lovemaking, infused with jasmine fragrances from the shaking braids of those wanton women, blow." Compare: "The winds, fragrant from the *saptacchada* trees, lovely from the white water lilies, sluggish from contact with brides who are wan from just making love, blow" (AŚ 122).
35. Ibid., 119. "Sighs" for the onomatopoetic *"sīt,"* a sound made by drawing in the breath to express rapture.
36. *Carpaṭapañcarikāstotra* (SG 11:281).
37. *Aparokṣānubhuti* 107.
38. MV 3.9–16; 16.81–92.

CHAPTER 6

1. AŚ 85.
2. Ibid., 67.
3. Ibid., 111.
4. Ibid., 38.
5. VCM 85.
6. AŚ 43.
7. Ibid., 30.
8. *Kenopaniṣadbhāṣya* (SG 3:65–101) 4.9.
9. VCM 322.
10. AŚ 69.
11. VCM 36.
12. Ibid., 81, 86, 161, 396.
13. Ibid., 559–560.
14. AG 74.
15. *Subhāṣitaratnakoṣa* of Vidyākara, ed. D. D. Kosambi and V. V. Gokhale (Cambridge, Mass., 1957), 1198.

HAWAII *Production Notes*

This book was designed by Roger Eggers. Composition and paging were done on the Quadex Composing System and typesetting on the Compugraphic Unisetter by the design and production staff of University of Hawaii Press.

The text and display typeface is Garamond No. 49.

Offset presswork and binding were done by Vail-Ballou Press. Text paper is Glatfelter Offset, basis 55.